FEMINIST READINGS / SERIES EDITOR: SUE ROE

Alfred Lord Tennyson

FEMINIST READINGS / SERIES EDITOR: SUE ROE

Alfred Lord Tennyson

MARION SHAW

Lecturer in English
University of Hull

HUMANITIES PRESS INTERNATIONAL, INC.
Atlantic Highlands, NJ

First published in 1988 in the United States of America by
HUMANITIES PRESS INTERNATIONAL, INC.,
Atlantic Highlands, NJ   07716

Library of Congress Cataloging-in-Publication Data

Shaw, Marion.
  Alfred Lord Tennyson.

  (Feminist readings)
  Bibliography: p.
  1. Tennyson, Alfred Tennyson, Baron, 1809–1892—
Criticism and interpretation.   2. Sex role in
literature.   3. Women in literature.   4. Men in
literature.   5. Love in literature.   I. Title.
II. Series.
PR5592.S47S5   1988   821'.8   88–21169
ISBN 0–391–03526–6
ISBN 0–391–03527–4 (pbk.)

Printed in Great Britain

For Liz and Cliff

Feminist Readings

Series Editor: Sue Roe

The *Feminist Readings* series has been designed to investigate
the link between literary writing and feminist reading by surveying the key works of English Literature by male authors from new
feminist perspectives.

Working from a position which accepts that the notion of
gender difference embraces interrelationship and reciprocity as
well as opposition, each contributor to the series takes on the
challenge of reassessing the problems inherent in confronting a
'phallocentric' literary canon, by investigating the processes involved in the translation of gender difference into the themes and
structures of the literary text.

Each volume surveys briefly the development of feminist literary
criticism and the broader questions of feminism which have been
brought to bear on this practice, from the initial identification of
'phallocentrism', through the tendency of early feminist critics to
read literature as a sociological document, through to feminist
criticism's current capacity to realign the discoveries of a wide
range of disciplines in order to reassess theories of gender difference. The tendency of the feminist critic to privilege texts
written by women and the notion that it might be possible to
identify an autonomous tradition of 'women's writing' can offer a
range of challenges to current feminist criticism, and the key texts
by male authors surveyed by the series are considered in this light.

Can there be a politics of feminist criticism? How might a
theory of sexual difference be seen to be directly applicable to
critical practice? The series as a whole represents a comprehensive survey of the development of various theories of gender
difference, and, by assessing their applicability to the writing of
the most influential male writers of the literary tradition, offers a
broadly revisionary interpretation of feminist critical practice.

Contents

Chronological Table

1809   (*6 August*) Alfred Tennyson born at Somersby, Lincolnshire, fourth child (of an eventual eleven children) of The Revd George Clayton Tennyson, Rector of Somersby, and Elizabeth (Fytche) Tennyson. T.'s childhood and youth were embittered by family feuds (his father was disinherited) and by his father's drunkenness and mental instability.

1816–20   Attended Louth Grammar School, which he hated. Subsequently educated at home by his father.

1827   *Poems by Two Brothers* (with elder brothers Frederick and Charles).
Entered Trinity College, Cambridge.

1829   Met Arthur Henry Hallam, also a student at Trinity College, who was to become T.'s close friend and the fiancé of his sister, Emily.
T. became a member of the 'Apostles', a Cambridge debating society, to which Hallam also belonged: a relatively happy time.

1830   *Poems, Chiefly Lyrical.*

1831   Death of T.'s father; T. left Cambridge without taking a degree.

1832   *Poems* (harshly criticized in *Quarterly Review*).

1833   Death of Hallam from cerebral haemorrhage whilst on holiday in Vienna.

1834–6	In love with and then disillusioned by Rosa Baring, daughter of a wealthy neighbour.
1837	T.'s family left Somersby. T. engaged to Emily Sellwood.
1840	Engagement to Emily broken off: beginning of several years of depression, ill health and financial insecurity.
1842	*Poems* (2 vols: vol. I revisions of previous poems, vol. II new poems).
1847	*The Princess*
1849	Renewed relationship with Emily Sellwood.
1850	*In Memoriam.* Married Emily Sellwood. Appointed Poet Laureate.
1852	Son Hallam born (followed by Lionel in 1854).
1853	Permanent home at Farringford, Isle of Wight (second home, Aldworth in Sussex, built in 1868).
1855	*Maud, and Other Poems.*
1859	*Idylls of the King* (i.e. 'Enid', 'Vivien', 'Elaine' and 'Guinevere'): final sequence completed 1885 with the publication of 'Balin and Balan' in *Tiresias, and Other Poems.*
1864	*Enoch Arden, etc.*
1875	*Queen Mary*, the first of seven plays.
1879	Publishes *The Lover's Tale* (written c.1830).
1883	Accepts the offer of a barony.
1886	Death of his son Lionel.
1889	*Demeter and Other Poems.*
1892	(*6 October*) T. died. (*28 October*) Posthumous publication of *The Death of Œnone, Akbar's Dream, and Other Poems.*

Select Bibliography

Text
The Poems of Tennyson, ed. Christopher Ricks (Longmans'
    Annotated English Poets), Longmans, Green Co., 1969; re-
    vised edition (incorporating the Trinity College Manuscripts) in
    three volumes, 1987.

Bibliography
Kirk H. Beetz, *Tennyson. A Bibliography, 1827–1982* (Scarecrow
    Author Bibliographies No. 68), Scarecrow Press, Metuchen, NJ
    and London, 1984.

Biography
[Hallam Lord Tennyson] *Alfred Lord Tennyson: A Memoir By His
    Son*, 2 vols., Macmillan, London, 1897
Charles Tennyson [T.'s grandson], *Alfred Tennyson*, Macmillan,
    London, 1949.
Robert B. Martin, *Tennyson: The Unquiet Heart*, Faber and
    Oxford University Press, London and New York, 1980.

Criticism
Jerome H. Buckley, *Tennyson: The Growth of a Poet*, Harvard
    University Press, Cambridge, Mass., 1960.
John Dixon Hunt (ed.), *Tennyson's 'In Memoriam': A Casebook*,
    Macmillan, London, 1970.
Wendell Stacy Johnson, *Sex and Marriage in Victorian Poetry*,
    Cornell University Press, Ithaca and London, 1975.
Gerhard Joseph, *Tennysonian Love: The Strange Diagonal*,
    University of Minnesota Press, Minneapolis, 1969.

John D. Jump (ed.), *Tennyson: The Critical Heritage*, Routledge & Kegan Paul, London, Barnes & Noble, New York, 1967.

John Killham, *Tennyson and 'The Princess': Reflections of an Age*, The Athlone Press, London, 1958.

John Killham (ed.), *Critical Essays on the Poetry of Tennyson*, Routledge & Kegan Paul, London, 1960.

Ralph W. Rader, *Tennyson's 'Maud': The Biographical Genesis*, University of California Press, Berkeley and London, 1963.

Joanna Richardson, *The Pre-Eminent Victorian: A Study of Tennyson*, Cape, London, 1962.

Christopher Ricks, *Tennyson* (Masters of World Literature Series), Macmillan, New York, 1972.

John D. Rosenberg, *The Fall of Camelot: A Study of Tennyson's 'Idylls of the King'*, Harvard University Press, Cambridge, Mass., 1973.

Edgar F. Shannon, *Tennyson and the Reviewers: A Study of His Literary Reputation and the Influence of the Critics upon His Poetry, 1827–1851*, Harvard University Press, Cambridge, Mass., 1952.

W.D. Shaw, *Tennyson's Style*, Cornell University Press, Ithaca and London, 1976.

Alan Sinfield, *The Language of Tennyson's 'In Memoriam'*, Blackwell, Oxford; Barnes & Noble, New York, 1971.

Alan Sinfield, *Alfred Tennyson* (Re-reading Literature Series), Blackwell, Oxford, 1986.

Acknowledgements

I wish to acknowledge the encouragement and advice of my friends, Angela Leighton and Patsy Stoneman, in the writing of this study, and also to express my gratitude to them as colleagues in the English Department at Hull University and particularly as fellow teachers on the 'Women and Literature' courses which are so rewarding a part of my working life. I also wish to thank the many students on those courses whose enthusiastic and creative feminism has endlessly stimulated and renewed my commitment to feminist criticism.

Introduction

The discourse of Absence is a text with two ideograms:
there are *the raised arms of Desire*, and
there are *the wide-open arms of Need*.
        (Roland Barthes, *A Lover's Discourse*)

Most feminist literary criticism has been and is concerned
with women's writing. For instance, although the Introduction to *Writing and Sexual Difference* (ed. Elizabeth
Abel, 1982) begins by stating that 'gender informs and
complicates both the writing and the reading of texts', the
book's first, summarizing article, by Elaine Showalter, takes
no account of the male gender and its writing and reading. In
surveying the tendencies and achievements of feminist
literary study since her own highly influential *A Literature of
Their Own* (1977), Showalter assumes that women's writing
is the central project of such study. As she defines it, this
project has developed theories of women's writing which
make use of 'four models of difference: biological, linguistic,
psychoanalytic, and cultural. Each is an effort to define and
differentiate the qualities of the woman writer and the
woman's text' (Showalter pp. 16–17; in Abel 1982). But
there are questions begged in this definition which relate
to the notion of 'difference': 'different' from what?; 'differentiated' by whom and for what purpose and according to
which norm? The answer to these questions lies, of course,
in male writing, and for feminist criticism to ignore this, or

1

to treat it merely as a point of reference unsusceptible or uninviting to investigation leads to a dangerous exclusivity. Women's writing is relational; it does not exist in some pure state of its own, in a country or a language of women's own making, but takes its nature as *women's* writing from its difference from men's. This is true also of men's writing but perhaps not in quite the same way, theirs being the master discourse which, although it certainly takes its very existence from not being female, looks not to what is 'inferior' for its conscious standards and distinctions but to its peers and forefathers.

There is also the question of access to and impact upon the culture of the dominant group. As Myra Jehlen has said, the problem with a feminist approach which is oppositional, where women's experience is taken as 'global', is that 'the issues and problems women define from the inside as global, men treat from the outside as insular, even parochial' (Jehlen p. 190; in Keohane, Rosaldo and Gelpi 1982). Such separatism leaves unscathed 'mainstream' critical practice and, by extension, literary production and the cultural process. It becomes a political bywater.

To swim in the mainstream, or perhaps *against* it, is, then, an inescapable requirement. In Jehlen's view, what is needed in feminist scholarship are ways of engaging with the dominant intellectual systems: 'since feminist thinking is the thinking of an insurgent group that in the nature of things will never possess a world of its own, such engagement would appear a logical necessity' (ibid. p. 191). With regard to literature, the 'dominant intellectual systems' are the male texts which largely constitute the canon, and the over-whelmingly male critical establishment, male not just in its personnel but in its assumptions of male norms and categories. A feminist engagement with these systems involves an investigation of the text and an appropriation of critical methodologies, in both cases from the perspective of gender relations; in other words, the sexual politics of the text and the sexual politics involved in the act of reading. In short, a woman's reading of a man's writing.

This brings me to Tennyson and to the kind of male writer

he is. The most successful of the Poet Laureates, the author of a number of extremely well-known and frequently anthologized poems such as 'The Charge of the Light Brigade' and 'The Lady of Shalott' (some of which are A-level texts), the epitome of Victorian respectability and the butt of the Modernists ('Alfred Lawn Tennyson', James Joyce called him), he seems to stand for all that is established, traditional, classic (to the point of parody) and authorized. He is a cultural phenomenon of some magnitude, endlessly investigated for his Victorian-ness whilst at the same time, as happens rather more with poets than with novelists, slipping the leashes of a historical placement to escape into 'universality'. In most criticism of his poetry his maleness has been overlooked, or rather it has been mistaken for a human absolute. Operating within a patriarchal poetic tradition, from the Greek writers whom he loved to emulate to his immediate Romantic predecessors, a tradition in which women were absent or, like Sappho, miraculous freaks, Tennyson as a 'great poet' has become desexed into representativeness of *all* humanity, his maleness the hidden figure in the 'reading of life' his poetry offers. A feminist reading ought to put the sex back into the text, to show the engendered and engendering nature of writing, to ask why such a man, precisely because he was a man, wrote in such a way at such a time. Such criticism becomes, particularly in the case of a classic writer like Tennyson, a process of demystification; the 'great poet' is located within sexual difference: after all, only a man, the second sex, no longer speaking for us or on our behalf (although certainly speaking to us and about us), our Other whose speech may seek to dominate and enclose but once perceived as Otherly may not do so by default.

This kind of criticism of a male text no longer primarily involves a put-down; the deliberate destructiveness of Kate Millett's *Sexual Politics* (1969), however necessary then in order to make us aware that texts are not innocent, neutral or objective in sexual terms, any more than they are in class, racial or religious ones, now seems outmoded. A later generation of feminist critics writing on male authors, Hilary

Simpson on D.H. Lawrence or Penny Boumelha on Hardy,
for instance, have been more concerned to contextualize and
comprehend the sexism of their authors than to condemn it.
Thus Simpson seeks to interpret Lawrence's writing 'in
relation to selected aspects of women's history and the
development of feminism' (Simpson 1982; p. 15) and
Boumelha to examine Hardy's fiction 'in the historical
situation that was a vital determination of his radicalism'
(Boumelha 1982; p. 8). This kind of criticism still maintains
a political purpose in the service of feminism, to an extent
Lillian S. Robinson refers to when she says, 'I am not
terribly interested in whether feminism becomes a
respectable part of academic criticism; I am very much
concerned that feminist critics become a useful part of the
women's movement' (Robinson 1971; p. 889). But being a
'useful part' means, I take it, becoming an investigator of the
problem of sexuality as it is mediated through works of
literature, rather than merely indicating the literature's
misogynist content. In these terms, a feminist reading of
Tennyson's poetry is, at the very least, an attempt to
understand gender relations in the Victorian period and
especially the constructs of masculinity and femininity (or,
what is not quite the same thing, manliness and
womanliness) which are a major part of its legacy to us.

The danger of a reading of this kind, as Lillian Robinson's
comment implies, is that it reduces literature, Tennyson's
poetry, to social history or sociology or a psychological case
study, or to something that is not literature. Ideally, a
feminist reading ought to be able to investigate the 'reality' of
the sexual politics of the text whilst at the same time
recognizing, and even illuminating, its fictiveness and
imaginative play. This smacks of trying to have one's cake
and eat it, both attacking and colluding with canonical law, a
disingenuity which Lillian Robinson accedes to when she
says, 'Radical criticism should be able to more than point out
a "correct line" on sex and class. Applying our analysis to
texts will determine . . . what it *means* to keep saying, "That
is a sexist book—but it's great literature"' (ibid.).

The ability, and the wish, to tolerate this double-think,

which seems to me inevitably involved in a feminist reading of classic male authors, derives in the first place from the woman critic's own cultural conditioning. Ever since I can remember, lines from 'The Lady of Shalott' have thrummed through my imagination, and at times of grief, fragments of *In Memoriam* spring unbidden to my mind in ways which I both distrust and am grateful for because they make a (male) artefact of my (female) experience. If I dismiss Tennyson, I dismiss my past; in any case, it cannot be done, I am in the possession of this voice from the past. What may be possible, what a feminist reading may effect, is an equalizing within this strange love relationship. This involves a critical impulse which has to do with an attraction between a female reader and male writing, a hetero-critical response which relates to the woman critic's desire to possess and interpret the male text in ways which give her satisfaction as a woman. Criticism of any kind seems to me to be a sexual activity, an intercourse of an intimate and appropriative kind; but in the erotics of criticism, there is a division into the homo-critical, where there is the search for sameness and lineage, for self-identity, and the hetero-critical, where otherness and opposition are sought, where the self is defined through difference. In respect of male writing, the feminist critical enterprise is, then, a quest for maleness within the text and also an inquiry into the constructedness of the male poetic voice, into that shaping and sustaining of an 'I' of poetic utterance which is sufficiently virile to take its place in a male poetic tradition. In recognizing how this construct comes about, one perceives not only how its existence derives from women's exclusion and diminution, but also how fragile and precarious are its exclusivity and aggrandizement.

Tennyson seems particularly to invite this kind of critical attention. It is not merely that, as Alan Sinfield has pointed out, there is a 'confusion of gender categories' (Sinfield 1986; p. 136) in Tennyson's poetry which is an invitation to think and talk and write yet once again about sexual relations, another turn of the screw of the (critical) discourse on sexuality, but also that there is a quality of vulnerability in Tennyson's exposure of himself to these confusions which makes his poetry desirable. As Sinfield puts it, Tennyson is 'playing a risky game, one which is likely to leave uncomfortable residues' (ibid.), and it is precisely this residual element, alluring in its uncomfortableness, which attracts a feminist critical reading. For there is a hope that in the residue, in what escapes from the safe game of writing and reading within unquestioned gender categories, there may be revealed the answers to two questions: what are men really like?; what do men want? To expect serious answers to these questions is to indulge the delusion of a Tiresias, but the asking of them is both exciting and enabling in that it makes of the woman critic the quester and the pursuer, the one who turns back in her flight from the encoding operations of her cultural conditioning to confront her captors. And there they all are: Milton and Wordsworth and Dickens, and aching Hardy and raging Lawrence—and needful, unsure Tennyson.

My feminist reading of Tennyson's poetry is the story of a love-story that fails. 'One has a profound, if irrational, instinct', Virginia Woolf wrote, 'in favour of the theory that the union of man and woman makes for the greatest satisfaction, the most complete happiness' (Woolf 1945; p. 96), and Tennyson would have agreed with her although he would not have included the word 'irrational' in the statement. In a world in which, as Carol Christ has expressed it, 'action has lost its religious imperative and seems to have gained meaning only from a Malthusian and Darwinian marketplace' (Christ p. 158; in Vicinus 1977), 'love', or what G.M. Young calls 'monogamic idealism about sex', becomes not just a refuge and inspiration in itself but also a paradigm of all the lost illusions of a commercial and industrial age. It is the Victorian version of pastoral. The pastoral fails because intrinsic to it is the 'irrational' and contradictory proposition that opposites, psychic as well as social, can be synthesized without loss of opposition. Tennyson's poetry explores and affirms this irrationality in a pessimistic progression towards the anti-pastoral. At the same time his poetry never ceases to yearn for the 'might-have-been', and this lyric longing struggles and resonates against all the explanations of failure and the displacements of anger and grief.

Tennyson was born in 1809, twenty-eight years before the reign of Victoria began, and he died in 1892, nine years before she died in 1901. During this long life-span, not only the changing face of the British landscape but also the patterns of social behaviour begin to assume a modern aspect. This is particularly true of the relations between the sexes. Tennyson's lifetime coincides with the trajectory of the marriage debate from the earnest reformism of the early period through the euphoria of the middle years to the disillusioned questioning of the last decades of the century. His lifetime was also, relatedly, an era of obsession with romantic love, and the period when feminism became an organized force with specific social and political aims. The age is vastly and articulately self-conscious about sexual relations and problematizes them in a manner which is very familiar to us. Tennyson's poetry contributes to and partakes of these problematics in its search for love, a search which is thwarted by the factors which make love desirable, that is, the differences between men and women.

My feminist reading of Tennyson's poetry is an attempt to track that search from its early romantic aspirations into the maze of contradictions which fracture its idealism. In this attempt I have used some of the insights of psycho-analysis, despite W.H. Auden's warning about Tennyson that 'No other poetry is easier, and less illuminating, to psychoanalyse' (Auden 1947; p. xiv). Auden was referring to what, even from the first, critics have recognized as 'an undercurrent of woe' in Tennyson's poetry so palpable as to make psychic investigation irresistible; certainly Auden himself could not resist the temptation. Auden's caution also relates to what, particularly in these post-structuralist days, is more generally perceived as the limitations, even the invalidity, of psychoanalytic criticism. Psychoanalysis offers a deciphering and interpretation of a text which proposes a 'truth' about it, a truth relating to an irreducible core of human action and psychic process. As Shoshana Felman says:

While literature is considered as a body of *language*—to be *interpreted*—psychoanalysis is considered as a body of *knowledge*, whose competence is called upon to *interpret*. Psychoanalysis, in other words, occupies the place of a *subject*, literature that of an *object*; the relation of interpretation is structured as a relation of master to slave . . . literature's function, like that of the slave, is to *serve* precisely the *desire* of psychoanalytic theory—its desire for recognition; exercising its authority and *power* over the literary field, holding a discourse of masterly competence, psychoanalysis, in literature, thus seems to seek above all its own *satisfaction*. (Felman 1982; pp. 5–6)

If psychoanalytic criticism enslaves literature in a relationship of so fundamentalist a kind, why use it as a critical method at all, and why, in particular, use it as a part of feminist criticism? Peter Brooks asks, 'What is *at stake* in the current uses of psychoanalysis?', and partly answers his own question by suggesting that what is at stake is our wish as critics to establish what Felman describes as the principle of *implication*:

We continue to dream of a convergence of psychoanalysis and literary criticism because we sense that there ought to be, there must be, some correspondence between literary and psychic process, that aesthetic structure and form, including literary tropes, must somehow coincide with the psychic structures they both evoke and appeal to. (Brooks 1987, in Rimmon-Kenan; p. 4)

From a feminist point of view, psychoanalysis, which is nineteenth-century, European, middle-class and male, seems to offer a likely mapping of nineteenth-century, middle-class, English, male poetry; and the converse. As discourses they implicate each other in maleness, and the feminist critic's role, to appropriate Felman's words, becomes that of 'a go-between' whose task it is 'to *generate implications* between literature and psychoanalysis—to explore, bring to light and articulate the various (indirect) ways in which the two domains do indeed *implicate each other*' (ibid. p. 9).

But perhaps there is more to it than this; yet another level of implication, that of the analyist/critic, is involved. In

discussing the reductiveness of Marie Bonaparte's psychoanalytic criticism of the short stories of Edgar Allan Poe,
Elizabeth Wright suggests that Bonaparte's analysis, for
all its shortcomings, nevertheless results in a 'compelling
fantasy, rather like a strange poem in its own right':

> This throws new light on the supposed reductiveness of
> psychoanalytic interpretation: the very reductiveness, instead of
> achieving the objectivity of which it was in search, reveals, in the
> intensity of its concentration, a subjective response given public
> articulation. (Wright 1984; pp. 44–5)

My feminist reading is a subjective response which seeks to
create just such a fantasy out of the convergence of psychoanalysis and Tennyson's poetry. The fantasy is of maleness
as power and need *in relation to women*, a fantasy in which
poetic expression and psychoanalytic theory are perceived as
deeply implicated. 'How easy it is to find what one is looking
for and what is occupying one's own mind', Freud wrote
(Freud 1959; p. 91), and what one finds everywhere, and
what one looks for everywhere, is women.

The basis of this feminist fantasy is the conviction that in
every society in every age men 'blame' women for their
mortal condition, for bringing them to life and therefore to
death, for teaching them desire and negation, fullness and
emptiness, love and hate. The balance of dread and yearning
in the gynophobia of this perpetual Fall-story varies according to the individual and his society; in the Victorian age the
tension between the perception of woman as all that was
desirable and all that was to be feared was particularly great.
My feminist reading sites Tennyson's poetry within this
tension and describes a process in which the lost female body
of earliest infancy is sought and mourned, and often loathed,
in a cycle of desire and frustration which is in fact unending
and insatiable, although I have brought it to rest in what I
interpret as a temporary reclamation of the maternal body in
the most homesick of all Tennyson's poems, *In Memoriam*.
The cycle begins in the notion of the twin-soul or sibling-
bond of Tennyson's early poetry of romantic love, particularly

The Lover's Tale, in which an undifferentiated and unified state of being is fantasized. The hopeless attempt to relate this idealization to the social arrangements of marriage and the ownership of property leads not only to the flight into the monstrous female stereotypes of patriarchal culture but also, perhaps more interestingly, into great uncertainty about male roles and insecurity about masculine identity. Fear of women and despair of marriage become increasingly present in Tennyson's poetry and culminate in the hysterical misogyny of 'Lucretius' and the austere advocacy of celibacy of *Idylls of the King*. This sexual extremism in Tennyson's women reduces his men to the nihilism of 'Enoch Arden' or the frail spirituality of King Arthur. In this fallen world of sexual difference, it is only through the mediating power of a secondary loss—the death of Arthur Hallam—which both compounds and articulates all earlier losses—that the primary and irreparable losses of childhood can be forgiven and accommodated. This constitutes an act of mourning which is the substance of *In Memoriam*.

My feminist reading is, then, an attempt to understand maleness as a function of poetic expression; and perhaps also to see poetic expression, particularly love poetry of the tradition to which Tennyson belonged, as a function of maleness. 'What poets . . . what poets they were!' Virginia Woolf exclaimed of Tennyson (and Christina Rossetti), and went on 'to wonder if honestly one could name two living poets now as great as [they] were then' (Woolf 1945; p. 16). The greatness Woolf laments is the 'humming' lyricism of their love poetry but although she regrets the loss of such poetry she also recognizes the cost it represents to human happiness and, particularly, to women's well-being. For the poems are a discourse of intense desire which takes its formulation from a polarized vision of human sexuality as all that is most depraved as well as most transcendent, and most necessary as well as most bothersomely gratuitous to all that makes us human.

SECTION A: LOVE AND MARRIAGE

CHAPTER ONE

Romantic Love

School parted us; we never found again
That childish world where our two spirits mingled
Like scents from varying roses that remain
One sweetness, nor can evermore be singled.
> (George Eliot, 'Brother and Sister')

They weren't brother and sister, but they were as fond
of each other as if they had been.
> (Hans Andersen, *The Snow Queen*)

Remind me how we loved our mother's body
our mouths drawing the first
thin sweetness from her nipples

our faces dreaming hour on hour
in the salt smell of her lap.
> (Adrienne Rich, 'Sibling Mysteries')

In Graham Greene's *A Gun for Sale*, at an important moment in the story, Raven, the hero, hears Tennyson's *Maud* on the radio, and later he remembers it as his death; the poem represents to him a romantic ideal, an impossible, redemptive love which reaches beyond death and denies human fallibility. As different a writer as Virginia Woolf also found *Maud* powerful for similar reasons; the love that *Maud* portrays is an illusion, of course, but one that is yet 'exciting, musical', strange yet familiar:

> The very reason why that poetry excites one to such
> abandonment, such rapture, is that it celebrates some feeling
> that one used to have . . . so that one responds easily, familiarly,
> without troubling to check the feeling. (Woolf 1945; p. 16)

Tennyson comes readily to mind as a poet of love; what
seems his most characteristic writing, when he is most
Tennysonian, is when he is writing about a kind of love that
is obsessive, total, idealistic and sublimatedly erotic:
romantic love. But it is a love which it is almost always
impossible to translate into marriage; the moral thrust of his
poems lies in a search for stability, domestic contentment
and social legitimacy yet their emotional charge depends on
the hopelessness of the lovers' predicament. Arthur says:

> ... for saving I be joined
> To her that is the fairest under heaven,
> I seem as nothing in the mighty world,
> And cannot will my will, nor work my work
> Wholly ...
> ('The Coming of Arthur', 84–8)

But his marriage fails, and Tennyson's longest poem, *Idylls
of the King*, like so many of his shorter ones, remains the
expression of an unrealizable ideal and an admission of the
irreconcilability of the intensities of romantic love with the
social exigencies of marriage.

A striking feature of many of Tennyson's love poems is
that the relationship they describe originates in childhood.
'Locksley Hall', *The Princess*, *Maud*, 'Enoch Arden' and
'Aylmer's Field' are amongst those in which the lovers have
either been affianced at birth or have grown up together as
cousins or childhood playmates. In other words, the
romantic love of adults in Tennyson's poems has its source in
affection of a quasi-sibling kind. Perhaps this is hardly
surprising in view of the social and educational arrangements
of the time. Most middle-class children in the nineteenth
century had little acquaintance with members of the opposite
sex outside their families. School for boys when they were
eight or nine, and for girls an enclosed, home-bound world,

ensured that intercourse between the sexes, unless it transgressed beyond the usual and proper, remained familial. Such limitation in the experience of the child and young adult inevitably led to an imaginative heightening of what heterosexual relationships the family could provide. In Victorian women's writing the lover whose appeal lay in fatherly dominance and maturity was a commonplace, and, as Ellen Moers has shown (Moers 1977; p. 105), girls' nursery relationships with their brothers resonated powerfully in adult women's imaginations from the Gothic fantasies of Emily Brontë and Christina Rossetti to the autobiographical realism of George Eliot.

The familial conditioning of men's heterosexual responses was no less powerful, but its focus, of course, was on mothers and sisters, particularly, it seems, on sisters. Dickens illustrates better than most authors a belief in sisters as typifying all that is good in women. Dickens's mothers are rarely good (or rarely present at all), but his sisters, like his daughters, who are sisters reborn, invariably are and they often take upon themselves the mothering role vacated by real mothers. Those women who will make good wives— Little Dorrit or Florence Dombey, for instance—establish proof of this by being excellent sisters and also by the sisterly relationship they have with their future husbands. Dickens's ideal love relationship is one in which the female is de-sexed, and what remains of her femininity is her caring and self-sacrificing regard for the male, whose own sexuality is thereby displaced, relegated to the underworld both of his own imagination and of Victorian society. In this divisive fantasy, mothers are inevitably ambivalently situated; economically and legally of no consequence, educationally inferior, and sexually fallen, they nevertheless occupy a position of the greatest imaginative significance as images of succour and purity. Dickens shelved the paradox by creating his mothers as absences; they never exist, like Pip's, or they die early, like David's, or else they are so obviously what a mother should never be, like Mrs Clenham in *Little Dorrit*, that they negatively posit an impossible ideal. Sisters, however, present no such problems; affectionate without being seductive, equal to their brothers whilst also serving them, stoic companions in adversity even as they solicit brotherly chivalry, they appear as figures of truce in the warfare between men and women, harbingers or relics of a golden world of romantic love and harmony.

Tennyson's childhood experiences were an exaggerated version, almost to the point of parody, of what we think of as typical nineteenth-century family life: a harsh father, kindly, ineffectual mother, ten brothers and sisters, assorted servants, cramped living conditions, and an emotional claustrophobia resulting from geographical isolation, a degree of poverty and the self-sufficiency that characterizes large families:

> So close were they that for years they hardly ever mixed with other children, since there were enough at home for almost any game they could invent. Knightly feats, jousting, and castles naturally occupied much of their outdoor play, and within doors they loved to write endless stories in letter form, the current instalment each night being slipped under the potato dish to be read aloud at the end of the meal. (Martin 1980; p. 23)

Such a combination of physical proximity and literary fantasy seems to have been a common feature of the large middle-class family: one is reminded of the Gondal and Angria worlds of the Brontës, of the Arnolds and their Fox How journal, and of Lewis Carroll, also one of eleven children, writing letter-stories to his sisters. The glimpses of Tennyson's loving relationship with his brothers and sisters, when 'he would take one child on his knee, put another between his legs in front of the fire, and prop two others against him on either side as he told them stories' (Martin 1980; p. 35), shine by contrast with the miseries of much else in his childhood: the loathed school at Louth he attended between the ages of seven and eleven, his father's increasing violence and drunkenness, the family's poverty and the bitterness of their disinherited position. His unhappiness was so great that many times during his boyhood he 'went out through the black night, and threw himself on a grave in the

churchyard praying to be beneath the sod himself'
(Tennyson 1897; I. 15).

Yet the notion of childhood contentment as a birthright
remained with Tennyson powerfully. One of his early poems
begins by claiming that 'From the East of life joybeams did
strike / On my young brows. Joy rose up like / White Venus,
whiter than all stars.' Christopher Ricks is surely right in
saying that 'those "joybeams" have rather a determined air'
(Ricks 1972; p. 16) and that they register Tennyson's
desperate wish to believe in childhood happiness rather than
evidence of his ever having experienced it. But the fact that
he desired it so much was an important factor in determining
Tennyson's whole concept of love and his location of its
origins in the 'rich foreshadowings' of the world of infancy.
In this respect he was very much part of his age, for his
lifetime coincided with a growing interest in the state of
childhood, both as a symbol of innocence and the life of the
imagination and as a matter of intense social, educational and
moral concern. As Peter Coveney has pointed out, the image
of the child dominates nineteenth-century literature and
becomes a focus for the century's dreams and fantasies as
well as for its discontents (Coveney 1967; pp. 91–110). In
questions of love, childhood becomes a standard by which
the holiness of the heart's affections are measured.

Tennyson's early education in the Classics, under the
fierce supervision of his father, brought him concepts
concerning a primordial happiness which confirmed and
gave literary authority to his childhood experience of
happiness lost or never consciously possessed. 'We live in the
world's ninth age', wrote Juvenal, lamenting a lost Golden
Age 'when the world was young, and the sky bright-new still
[and] men lived differently'. In his reading of the English
Romantic poets, Tennyson saw this blessed 'ancient state'
recovered from the legendary and mythical to become a
stage, albeit a vestigial one, in human life, childhood:
'Heaven lies about us in our infancy!'. But the child in early
Romantic poetry, particularly in Wordsworth, is solitary;
the boy listening to the owls or rowing across the lake, or
Blake's laughing child on a cloud, are alone. What constitutes

their blessedness is their unstained receptivity to nature's teachings:

> When couched in Boyhood's passionless tranquillity,
> The natural mind of man is warm and yielding,
> Fit to receive the best impressions ...
> 　　　　(*The Devil and the Lady*, III.II.176–8)

This is fourteen-year-old Tennyson, prodigiously and half-jokingly echoing Romantic sentiments. When he comes to treat the notion of a lost happiness seriously, however, such definitions will not suffice. For him, as for the later Romantic poets and for the nineteenth century in general, happiness is not merely innocence, it is also love, and love of a particular kind. In one respect it is a love which, in the words of Aristophanes in Plato's *Symposium*, 'restores us to our ancient state by attempting to weld two beings into one and to heal the wounds which humanity suffered ... love is simply the name for the desire and pursuit of the whole.' At the same time, for Tennyson this desired wholeness involves a pre-lapsarian state of innocence which only the world of childhood can provide. As Shelley had shown, childhood love, particularly of a consanguineous kind, provides a paradigm not merely for sympathetic connection but also for spiritual completion. 'Would we two had been twins of the same mother!', cries the lover in 'Epipsychidion', 'For in the fields of Immortality / My spirit should at first have worshipped thine ... Or should have moved beside it on this earth, / A shadow of that substance, from its birth.' And as Peter Thorslev has shown, incestuous love of this kind symbolizes the poet's 'narcissistic sensibility, or, more philosophically speaking, his predilection for solipsism' (Thorslev 1965; p. 50).

　　Tennyson treats the theme of incest more circumspectly. In his childhood love relationships he invokes the emotional and physical intimacy which belongs to the nursery, yet by making his child-lovers cousins or neighbours—as in the case of 'Locksley Hall', *Maud*, 'Enoch Arden' and 'Aylmer's Field', for example—he leaves open the possibility that the

sensuous purity of their early affection can be decorously
transformed into an adult love, can miraculously overcome
the problems of sexual experience. There is the suggestion
throughout all Tennyson's love poetry that if a boy is reared
in the innocent and reciprocal love of a 'sister' whom he may
at some time properly marry, then the evils of profligacy and
degeneracy will never assail him:

> for indeed I knew
> Of no more subtle master under heaven
> Than is the maiden passion for a maid,
> Not only to keep down the base in man,
> But teach high thought, and amiable words
> And courtliness, and the desire of fame,
> And love of truth, and all that makes a man.
> ('Guinevere', 474–80)

But in neither Shelley nor Tennyson is romantic love able to
develop into marriage, and why this is so relates to the notion
of 'twinning' which lies at the heart of this kind of love.
Modern attempts to understand the psychology of romantic
love have built on the ancient classical notions of it as both a
lost state and a 'desire and pursuit of the whole', and have
incorporated into this the Romantic idea that this perfect
state can be glimpsed within our own lives, that love is a
nostalgic impulse towards some earlier state, what Freud
calls a 'homesickness'. In these definitions there is the
recognition that romantic love has more to do with the Self
than with a relationship between two individuals, and with
a Self that has existed, or is believed to have existed, in
the past, in the '"far, far away" [that] had always a strange
charm' for Tennyson. In Shulamith Firestone's blunt words,
romantic love is a regressively infantile search for a state of
ego security which is 'the height of selfishness: the self
attempts to enrich itself through the absorption of another
being' (Firestone 1972; p. 123).

Firestone's argument is based on Simone de Beauvoir's
bitter chapter on 'The Woman in Love' in *The Second Sex*
and confirms her view that 'love, perhaps even more than
childbearing, is the pivot of women's oppression today'

(Firestone 1972; p. 121). De Beauvoir's argument, arrived at through a formidable combination of existentialist philosophy and a reading of Freud and Lacan, postulates a definition of love as 'an identification with the loved one' but an identification which psychologically attempts to supply whatever has been lost in the socializing process the infant and child undergoes. For de Beauvoir, this experience of being 'in love' is very different for a man and a woman; this difference, however, 'has nothing to do with the laws of nature. It is the difference in their situations that is reflected in the difference men and women show in their conceptions of love' (de Beauvoir 1987; p. 653).

This line of argument is profitably developed by Juliet Mitchell in her essay on 'Romantic Love' in which she attempts to define the psychological characteristics of such love more rigorously, and, what neither de Beauvoir nor Firestone were concerned with, to analyse the nature of the difference between men's and women's conception of love, particularly as that conception is expressed in literature. In Mitchell's view, romantic love harks back to an infant self which is pre-genital:

> It is only with genital love and the implication of the tabooed, incestuous love for the parents that love and sexuality take on their meaning of interpersonal relationships—that is, love between people. Before this particular juncture, sexual feelings are from a body point of view, auto-erotic and imaginatively narcissistic. Furthermore, this pre-Oedipal infant does not have a body-ego or self that in psychological terms, it meaningfully, or symbolically, distinguishes as masculine or feminine. This pre-Oedipal child is psychologically bisexual. It seems to me that it is exactly this area of pre-interpersonal sexuality that we are talking about in the case of romantic love. . . . Romantic love is about the self, it is erotic, but does not have a sexual object that is ultimately different from itself. The lady of the courtly epic, Goethe's eternal female, Cleo the poet's muse, the feminine principle of *fin de siècle* artists are all, in the last resort, metaphors for the lost female part of the original, psychologically bisexual self. (Mitchell 1984; pp. 110–11)

As Mitchell points out, according to this psychological model, romantic love, because it is pre-interpersonal, is nonprocreative and therefore nihilistic: 'being only about the individual, [it] is the triumph of death over life.' The antithesis of this is interpersonal love, what de Beauvoir calls 'authentic love' which recognizes 'the contingence of the other with all his idiosyncrasies, his limitations, and his basic gratuitousness' (de Beauvoir 1987; p. 664). This kind of love, Mitchell says, is 'procreative', 'legitimate', and 'the triumph of sexuality over death, the species over the individual'. In literary representation, which articulates our fantasy lives rather more than our social realities, this kind of interpersonal love has, as narrative, been directed towards marriage, and its treatment is usually comic. Romantic love, on the other hand, is placed outside marriage, as adultery or star-crossed courtship, and its depiction is tragic or at least pathetic. Love-stories of this kind are usually the province of male writers because, Mitchell suggests, of the different nature of a man's relationship to his pre-Oedipal narcissistic self. The primary narcissism of girls and boys, which in the first place is not essentially different, and which is psychologically re-entered in romantic love, undergoes a different fate in the socializing process each sex experiences. To succeed socially, the girl must repeat the narcissism of her earliest phase in order to become an attractive sexual object to men, to obtain a husband. Thus for her, the search in romantic love for completion becomes a social acceptability, marriage: 'the narcissism of her romantic love is the mark of her attractiveness ... [her] bisexuality is externalized in finding, quite literally, another half with which to complete [herself].' For the boy, however, narcissism is regressive. For social success, he must look outwards towards action, power and the possession of others, not inwards awaiting his completion by another. Romantic love for men is socially negative; its regressive nature has no social value and if persisted in can lead only to the individual's extinction. Men's residual narcissism finds expression, in literature and sometimes in life, in nostalgia or in a movement towards death: romantic love for men 'looks backwards, or if it looks forward, it looks only to death'. So, generally speaking, and with *Wuthering Heights* an interesting exception, romance

literature by women, or written with women primarily
in mind, is of the love-and-marriage type; the literature
of *liebestod* is written by men. Both kinds of writing, as
de Beauvoir and Firestone were aware, confirm women's
dependency, either by emphasizing the centrality of love and
marriage to women's lives or by idealizing false notions
concerning the absolute nature of love.

If romantic love is self-love which 'offers the neglected
possibilities of the other sex that are always contained within
every human being', and if this vestigial drive has its origins
in the bisexual and auto-erotic state of earliest infancy, then
Tennyson's location of the origins of his tragic love-stories
in childhood intimacy is a disconcertingly literal exposure
of the infantile nature of Romantic love. But this should not
be particularly surprising when one considers how the
history of romantic love has shown that its finest expressions
have coincided with social arrangements which, however
obliquely, have legitimized infantile incest. The Mariolatry
and the adoration of the lost unattainable mother-lady of
Troubadour poetry, or the mother-Queen worship of English
Renaissance writing, take their emotional resonance from
this kind of transgressively familial feeling. In the nineteenth
century the idealization of childhood, and an accompanying
sanctification of motherhood, make available a variant of the
discourse of infantile incestuous sexuality which is the
substance of romantic love. Love-and-childhood becomes
for Tennyson, as for so many of his generation, the locus of a
lost content, the domain of residual emotion which romantic
love inhabits and which is both solace for and justification of
the harsh materialism of the adult world.

Tennyson's enduring obsession with nursery love makes
its first and most revealing appearance in a work 'written in
my nineteenth year', *The Lover's Tale*. Although Tennyson
withdrew this poem from publication in 1832 as 'too full of
faults', it is a powerful and characteristic piece of writing, as
he recognized in eventually allowing it to be published,
revised with an additional fourth section, in 1879. Such
hoarding and reworking of unpublished material was not
untypical of Tennyson; as Christopher Ricks has argued,

Tennyson's self-borrowing was 'not a convenience but a cast of mind' (Ricks 1967; p. 225), and it usually indicated a psychic anxiety of nagging persistence which, as in the case of *The Lover's Tale*, could only be resolved with difficulty and awkwardness and after many years. Tennyson claimed that the poem was based on a tale from Boccaccio (*Decameron*, Day X, Novel 4). In fact, it is only the fourth, much later section, 'The Golden Supper', which makes use of the Boccaccio tale and the evidence suggests that the first three sections, some 1,500 lines in length, were not written with such a conclusion in mind but, like much of Tennyson's early verse, are little concerned with the sort of narrative Boccaccio provides but are remarkable for their depiction of states of yearning or anxiety. In this case, the poem enacts a psychic drama concerning childhood love and the madness which follows the withdrawal of that love.

The urgency of Tennyson's attraction to this theme can be seen by comparing *The Lover's Tale* with a much shorter work by a poet who influenced the young Tennyson strongly, Byron's 'The Dream'. In this poem the story of 'a maiden and a youth' is given as a dream which changes, with cinematic effect, from one scene to another recounting how the boy loves his adopted sister—'he had ceased / To live within himself; she was his life, / The ocean to the river of his thoughts, / Which terminated all'—but to the girl 'he was / Even as a brother—but no more.' The couple separate, the girl to marry, to become unhappy and finally to go mad, the boy to become an outcast. The poem concludes with an admission of the inexplicable yet 'real' import of this dream:

> It was of a strange order, that the doom
> Of these two creatures should be thus traced out
> Almost like a reality—the one
> To end in madness—both in misery.
>
> (203–6)

This echoes the poem's opening description of the 'wide realm of wild reality' that belongs to the world of sleep in which dreams both recall the lost impulses of the past and

also, by becoming 'a portion of ourselves', act as 'Sibyls of the
future.' The poem thus strikingly locates its story of lost
childhood love in the unconscious mind which governs
sleeping:

> [Dreams] shake us with the vision that's gone by,
> The dread of vanished shadows—Are they so?
> Is not the past all shadow?—What are they?
> Creations of the mind?—The mind can make
> Substance, and people planets of its own
> With beings brighter than have been, and give
> A breath to forms which can outlive all flesh.
>   (16–22)

Tennyson replaces this dream opening with an invocation to
memory, 'Goddess of the Past . . . great Mistress of the ear
and eye', delivered by Julian, the lover, who tells his tale to
companions—'See, sirs, / Even now . . .'—as a retrospect on
his childhood and youth. By this means, the poem authenti-
cates its own fantasy; this is memory, not dream, it is history,
autobiography told to witnesses, not the 'strange order' of
Byron's poem. Tennyson has interestingly reversed the
process; in *The Lover's Tale* the story of unconscious desire
is located in the world of childhood experience, unlike
Byron's poem where childhood rapture is more safely
explained as an aspect of dreaming. The greater intensity of
his story is conveyed by the closer relation Tennyson
establishes between the children in his poem; Julian and
Camilla* are cousins born in the same hour, children of
sisters and reared together by his mother and her father,
their other parents having died. They are as close as twins
but without the overt incest prohibition actual twinship
would incur. Their infancy licenses a total physical intimacy
of an erotic nature more pronounced and specific than
Byron's shadowy dream-scenes offer:

---

* 'Cadrilla' in the original version; I have followed Christopher Ricks (*The Poems of
Tennyson*, 1969) in using Tennyson's revision.

>   one soft lap
> Pillowed us both: a common light of eyes
> Was on us as we lay: our baby lips,
> Kissing one bosom, ever drew from thence
> The stream of life, one stream, one life, one blood,
> One sustenance ...
>   ...   we slept
> In the same cradle always, face to face.
> Heart beating time to heart, lip pressing lip,
> Folding each other, breathing on each other,
> Dreaming together (dreaming of each other
> They should have added), till the morning light ...
> Falling, unsealed our eyelids, and we woke
> To gaze upon each other.
>   (I.229–60)

What Julian narrates is a fantasy of completion, what
Aristophanes calls 'our primitive condition when we were
wholes': Self delightedly gazing on Other before it has
become Otherly, whilst it still remains Self, before auto-
erotic bisexuality has given way to genital sexual opposition.
But this is, of course, an impossible state, so totally beyond
consciousness that it cannot be remembered but only
imagined or dreamed. In imagination Julian can dwell on its
ecstasies—'At thought of which my whole soul languishes /
And faints, and hath no pulse, no breath'—but it lies beyond
recall, beyond language:

> Why in the utter stillness of the soul
> Doth questioned memory answer not, nor tell
> Of this our earliest, our closest-drawn,
> Most loveliest, most delicious union?*
>   (I.270–3)

Julian's hope had been that this ideal state could be
protracted into maturity, the sister become the wife, but
Camilla had rejected him for his friend Lionel. In a manner

---

* In the revisions of 1879 Tennyson neutralized the eroticism of this line by
changing it to 'Most loveliest, earthly-heavenliest harmony'.

similar to the hero's descent into madness in *Maud*, Julian
entered a nightmare world of phantasmagoric marriages and
funerals so painful to recall that the narrative of these past
events ends abruptly. His tale represents the delusion of the
romantic lover that self-love can be made to perform a
procreative, interpersonal and social function, that although
outside time it can also submit to the processes of time.
Julian's anguished questions—

> Why were we one in all things, save in that
> Where to have been one had been the cope and crown
> Of all I hoped and feared?—if that same nearness
> Were father to this distance, and that *one*
> Vauntcourier to this *double*? if Affection
> Living slew Love . . . ?
>
> (II.25–30)

are unaswerable, at least as far as the early version of *The
Lover's Tale* is concerned, because the poem's faulty assumption is that the idealistic love of romantic fantasy, in
which 'the object serves as a substitute for some unattained
ego ideal of our own' (Freud 1955b; p. 112), can be
converted to 'affectionate' love without any modifying
inhibition of aim. The only true course of action that Julian
as lover can follow is that leading to destruction, to his own
death and that of Camilla. But this is not what happens in
The Lover's Tale. In the first place, Camilla does not
recognize the nature of Julian's love for her and cannot
participate in the fantasy it entails; she treats Julian as a
brother in whom she can confide her love for another man.
But more importantly, there is an inhibition, perhaps even a
prohibition, at work in the poem which prevents the extreme
conclusions which the lover's tale should logically lead to.
Julian fantasizes about his and Camilla's death, but even
here, in the fantasy within the fantasy of the poem, he cannot
do so in satisfactorily romantic terms; in his dreams his dead
love eludes him—'her weight / Shrank in my grasp . . . I,
groaning, from me flung / Her empty phantom' (II.199–
203)—and he is left alone 'beside the empty bier'. This early

version of *The Lover's Tale* ends inconclusively in neither life nor death, and Tennyson refused to publish it.

He revised it and published it in 1879, nearly fifty years after its conception. He also made the important addition of the final fourth section, 'The Golden Supper' (which he had published separately in 1870), in which the narrator is changed from Julian, the lover of the first three sections, to 'Another' who retells the Boccaccio tale in which a man who has long loved a married lady finds her mistakenly left for dead by her family. He restores her to health, gives her brotherly protection during her confinement and then behaves most nobly by restoring her and her child to her joyful husband, not without some riddling over her identity. Such an addition to *The Lover's Tale* has generally been regarded as 'an incongruous conclusion' (Martin 1980; p. 161) and indeed there is an abrupt narrational and stylistic change; the poem moves out of the claustrophobic, solipsistic world of the lover into a more austere, observed world of social relations. But the very incongruity of the ending represents a triumph in the development of Tennyson's obsessive concern with the subject of romantic love, a register of how resolved or abandoned he now considered the issue to be. After completing *The Lover's Tale* he wrote no further love-and-marriage poems.

Boccaccio's tale provided Tennyson with a version of the Sleeping Beauty story which he had used in earlier poems such as 'Mariana', 'The Day-Dream', 'The Lady of Shalott' and even *The Princess*. In these poems the 'dead' maiden requires the lover's kiss to waken her from a frozen state of romantic idealization. In 'The Golden Supper', this awakening is given in poetry which deliberately evokes a tradition of writing about romantic love, and also a tradition of Romantic poetry, from *Romeo and Juliet* through Keats to Tennyson's own *Maud*:

> But, placing his true hand upon her heart,
> 'O, you warm heart,' he moaned, 'not even death
> Can chill you all at once:' then starting, thought
> His dreams had come again. 'Do I wake or sleep?

Or am I made immortal, or my love
Mortal once more?' It beat—the heart—it beat:
Faint—but it beat: at which his own began
To pulse with such a vehemence that it drowned
The feebler motion underneath his hand.

(IV. 74–82)

But this impulse towards a belated romantic idealization is immediately cancelled. Married to another man, and pregnant by him, Camilla returns to the social obligations of marriage and motherhood more directly and starkly than in any of the other Sleeping Beauty poems. But if Camilla finds her position resolved, Julian, the lover, finds in this transition his own denial. His 'love' cannot move beyond an autoeroticism which paradoxically renders him, in a different sense of the word, unloving and unlovable. The only love possible for such a figure as Julian is 'a maternal substitute who would cling to his body like a poultice—a reassuring balm ... a permanent wrapping' (Kristeva 1986; p. 251). This is a love which Julian's narcissistic nostalgia had evoked at the beginning of the poem—'one soft lap / Pillowed us both ... our baby lips / Kissing one bosom'—, and although this maternal scene is now briefly recaptured, even approaching the point of re-entry into a state of primal union—the imagery of 'heart beating time to heart' of line 254 (quoted p. 25 above) in section one is recalled—, it must now be recognized as fantasy; 'Ay, but you know that you must give me back', says Camilla. Wakened into time and interpersonality, the dream of romantic love, in the scheme of the poem, is abruptly forced to give way to affectionate love. The divided and oppositional nature of the two is here emphasized by their representation in different characters; the husband Lionel usurps the lover Julian who now passes 'for ever from his native land' in a final line of the poem which recalls, whilst it also rejects, that 'native land of Love' the opening sections of *The Lover's Tale* have celebrated.

Several of Tennyson's poems work over material and themes from *The Lover's Tale*, but in none of them, with the exception of *The Princess*, does romantic love lead to

marriage, nor does it become an end in itself, that is, find a
resolution in *liebestod*. Even *Maud*, although it is bejewelled
with the iconography of romantic love and toys with a
romantic ending in which 'sullen-seeming Death may give /
More life to Love than is or ever was / In our low world'
(I.644–46), does not fully carry out its romantic intentions.
Although the poem diagnoses the romantic and nihilistic
impulses as cognate, its chivalric purpose wavers towards the
poem's conclusion: Maud's roses and lilies are exchanged
for, not consummated in, 'the blood-red blossom of war with
a heart of fire'. Of all Tennyson's poems, *Maud* possesses the
finest writing about romantic love, perhaps the finest of any
writing in the nineteenth century, yet is is not truly a love
poem but an oddly hybrid work in which a vortex of romantic
feeling is encircled by contingent but irrelevant 'explanations',
a palimpsest in which an overtext of extraneous material fails
to resolve or disguise the problems of what lies beneath. The
hybridism results, as in *The Lover's Tale*, from Tennyson's
use of earlier material, his revisiting of his past, the past of
the youthful poet seeking his (imagined) past, nostalgia upon
nostalgia in an ever-recessive movement.

This particular flight back to his origins occurred at a
time (*Maud* was published in 1855) when Tennyson had
left behind the poverty of his youth to become a man
of substance and property, a husband and father, and a
public figure as Poet Laureate. His political attitudes of this
period, pseudonymously expressed in brash newspaper
poems attacking Britain's appeasement policy towards Louis
Napoleon, were highly patriotic and militaristic, anti-com-
mercial and anti-democratic:

> Though niggard throats of Manchester may bawl,
>   What England was, shall her true sons forget?
> We are not cotton-spinners all,
>   But some love England and her honour yet.
>   ('The Third of February, 1852', 43–6)

It was against this background that *Maud* was written, with
untypical swiftness on the crest of excitement generated by

another event which intensified Tennyson's sense of class
and national identity, the Crimean War. But the urgent
topicality of the poem overlays a relic from Tennyson's past
around which the poem is constructed, a lyric written in
1833–4, 'Oh! that 'twere possible'. This had been written
soon after Arthur Hallam's death at a time when Tennyson's
grief and loneliness were intense. Although he published it in
1837, he did so reluctantly, 'cobbling up an ending for it'
(Rader 1963; p. 6) to please a friend, and subsequently
regarding it as incomplete. Like the first unpublished
version of *The Lover's Tale*, the lyric represents an emotional need which Tennyson could not forget or abandon and
which waited to be satisfied or exorcized by changed personal
or social circumstances. The patriotic fervour of the Crimean
War years, and Tennyson's increasing hostility towards
laissez-faire commercialism, provided the circumstances
necessary to complete the lyric.

Yet it would be truer to say that *Maud* effects a containment of the lyric rather than a completion or resolution. And
in a sense, Tennyson did not ever quite finish with the lyric;
although he did not actually use it again, or its theme of the
hopelessness of desire, he remained, as Ralph Rader has
shown, curiously excited about *Maud* for the rest of his life,
and he rehearsed its paradoxes through the repeated readings
he gave of the poem:

> There was a peculiar freshness and passion in his reading of
> *Maud*, giving the impression that he had just written the poem,
> and that the emotion which created it was fresh in him. This had
> an extraordinary influence on the listener, who felt that the
> reader had been *present* at the scenes he described, and that he
> still felt their bliss or agony. (Tennyson 1897; II.409, quoted
> Rader 1963; p. 2)

'Oh! that 'twere possible' repeats the division established in
The Lover's Tale between a dream state of perfect union
which restores the lover to a state 'sweeter, sweeter / Than
anything on earth' (9–10) and a 'death-like type of pain' in
which he is abandoned in a nightmare world of isolation:

> I loathe the squares and streets,
> And the faces that one meets,
> Hearts with no love for me.
>   (58–60)

In his use of this lyric twenty years later in *Maud*, Tennyson did not simply tack on new narrative material as he had done in *The Lover's Tale*. 'Oh! that 'twere possible' lies at the heart of the new poem, buried within its social commentary and even within its love-story. It is almost as though the rest of the poem were written to explain, to cover up, finally to have done with, the unassuageable anguish and yearning of this early lyric of romantic love. The mental instability of the protagonist and the corrupt society he lives in, the feuding families and the quarrel with the brother, Maud's death and the protagonist's departure for the war, are evidence produced to show that this kind of love cannot survive the harshnesses of its economic environment. But this evidence is a kind of displacement of the blame for the failure of love onto social causes, to conceal the flaw that 'Oh! that 'twere possible', in its linkage of loss and eroticism, and in its very irresolution and incompletion, had already implicitly acknowledged:

> Oh! that 'twere possible,
>   After long grief and pain,
> To find the arms of my true-love
>   Round me once again!
>   (1–4)

But it is not possible, or only in death, or in a dream, or in the fantasy of romantic love which haunts Tennyson's poetry well into his maturity, an infantile spectre of powerful erotic intensity never completely exorcized but merely laid aside or covered over. 'Oh! that 'twere possible', which Tennyson admitted was his most 'touching' poem (Tennyson 1897; II.466), rehearses the irresolvably dichotomous dilemma of the lover in *The Lover's Tale* of either total (and unattainable) absorption into the loved object or the total social alienation of an unmirrored narcissistic self. The fury and violence of the 'narrative' of *Maud* are a substitutive recognition of this appalling dilemma; otherwise incongruous as social criticism, they operate as transference for the pain and disillusionment with which, for Tennyson, 'Oh! that 'twere possible' after twenty years still resonated.

It was in 'Aylmer's Field' (published in 1864) that Tennyson finally attempted to rewrite *The Lover's Tale*, this time, apparently, fulfilling the conditions of the romantic love-story. Edith and Leolin, like Camilla and Julian, are childhood playmates and share an 'immemorial intimacy' of youthful companionship:

> So these young hearts not knowing that they loved . . .
> Gathered the blossom that rebloomed, and drank
> The magic cup that filled itself anew.
>
> (134–43)

As the poem makes clear, when love grows from the 'dear familiarities of dawn', it ought to become 'master of all', even of the harsh social exigencies—she is heiress to a landowner, he is a poor rector's orphan—which obstruct it and which ensure in the lovers' deaths the failure of the relationship in social terms and its 'success' as a romance. But it isn't quite as simple as this; Leolin is more like a husband than a lover (it is significant that his name is similar to the husband's in *The Lover's Tale*), the lovers' union is perceived by disinterested onlookers as entirely suitable, and both Leolin and Edith have social obligations outside their love, he in the law, she in charity work. There is little doubt that theirs would have been, in all senses, a fruitful marriage. In fact, although 'Aylmer's Field' establishes the preconditions for the 'completion' of romantic love in death, and on an actual narrative level achieves this, the interest of the poem swerves away from this event—a mere twenty lines are given to the joint deaths of the lovers—towards an attack of exceptional rhetorical violence upon the greed, family pride and class snobbery which have prevented the lovers' marriage. The lesson of the poem is that unless innocent love such as Edith's and Leolin's is allowed to develop into marriage and the birth of children, then chaos and dissolution, or at least the 'barren open field' the title refers to, will ensue. It is an extreme conclusion and, indeed, there is generally in 'Aylmer's Field' an extremism and indecorum of style sufficiently striking to suggest that social and psychic anxieties have become confused, or, rather, that they have become unbalanced. In the development from *Maud*, romantic love is now seen as almost completely an irrelevance, an admittedly infantile or idyllic dream to be despatched with the melodramatic ruthlessness of Leolin's suicide. In the emotional void this leaves behind there is a kind of implosion of Tennyson's Carlylean conservatism and his post-Darwinian pessimism:

>   I wished my voice
> A rushing tempest of the wrath of God
> To blow these sacrifices through the world—
> Sent like the twelve-divided concubine
> To inflame the tribes: but there—out yonder—earth
> Lightens from her own central Hell—O there
> The red fruit of an old idolatry—
> The heads of chiefs and princes fall so fast,
> They cling together in the ghastly sack—
> The land all shambles—naked marriages
> Flash from the bridge, and ever-murdered France,
> By shores that darken with the gathering wolf,
> Runs in a river of blood to the sick sea.
>   (756–68)

In 'Aylmer's Field' the complementarity between romantic love and the economic realities it is supposed to palliate and justify has broken down. In writing like this (for one might ask of the quoted passage what relevance the Levite's concubine and the French revolution have to Edith and Leolin) Tennyson is in danger of collapsing the ideological structures within which romantic love, and the writing of love poetry, operate. A violent randomness, already at work in *Maud*, is fully exercised in 'Aylmer's Field'; what keeps it from anarchy and incoherence is the relation of this displaced anger to something that does not occur in the poem (or, significantly, only in an etiolated form in the Aylmer parents), and that is marriage. Anxiously regarded, held at bay as an untested proposition, marriage as absent hope in 'Aylmer's Field' is all that remains to keep the structures of society in place.

In a subtle distinction between the narcissist and the auto-eroticist, Kristeva sees the narcissist as someone with a potential for love, unlike the auto-eroticist who 'has neither an other nor an image'. The lover, she implies, is a narcissist on the point of growing up; unlike the romantic lover, the lover proper is a 'narcissist with an *object* ... there is an idealizable other who returns his own ideal image (that is the narcissistic moment), but he is nevertheless an other' (Kristeva 1986; p. 250). Tennyson's protagonists up to and including *Maud* experience the narcissistic moment but they cannot move away from it, neither backwards into auto-eroticism, which would be death, nor forwards into recognition of the image as other. They are left in a kind of limbo, neither romantic nor authentic lovers.

What delivers Tennyson from the stasis of this psychological dilemma is a side-step movement into an advocacy of marriage, not married love but marriage as an institution. The narcissist's 'object' remains undiscovered but its absence is supplied by an idea of marriage as a whole set of rules, obligations and metaphoric applications which constitute a different discourse from the discourse of love which seemed to be his concern. 'Aylmer's Field' illustrates the switch in process. In the context of Tennyson's long ongoing poem about marriage, *Idylls of the King*, where it occurs about midway, before the more pessimistic books such as 'Pelleas and Ettarre' and 'The Last Tournament' were written, it represents a stage in Tennyson's growing concern, which he will develop to its conclusions in *Idylls of the King*, with marriage as a social absolute and his sense of the irrelevance of romantic love to this inflexible and exacting institution. In the marriage poem of his middle period, *The Princess*, the need to conceptualize marriage as a communion—'the two-celled heart beating, with one full stroke'—seemed to demand the transcendence and idealism that romantic love could supply. Yet to attempt in such a way

to use the psychic energies of romantic love to fortify the
social requirements of marriage was to embrace a contradiction, one which even *The Princess* acknowledges. It was
also in an attempt to accommodate this contradiction, and at
the same time to harness his nostalgia to social ends, that
Tennyson yoked together the early and late parts of *The
Lover's Tale*. It is his final word on the subject of romantic
love wherein it is delivered over and laid to rest within the
'charmed circle' of marriage:

> . . . the widower husband and dead wife
> Rushed at each other with a cry, that rather seemed
> For some new death than for a life renewed;
> Whereat the very babe began to wail;
> At once they turned, and caught and brought him in
> To their charmed circle . . .
> . . . —the sight of this
> So frighted [Julian], that turning to me
> And saying, 'It is over: let us go'— . . .
> He past for ever from his native land.
>   (IV.369–84)

CHAPTER TWO

Marriage

What marriage may be in the case of two persons of cultivated faculties, identical in opinions and purposes, between whom there exists that best kind of equality, similarity of powers and capacities with reciprocal superiority in them ... I will not attempt to describe.... But I maintain, with the profoundest conviction, that this, and this only, is the ideal of marriage; and that all opinions, customs, and institutions which favour any other notion of it ... are relics of primitive barbarism. The moral regeneration of mankind will only really commence, when the most fundamental of the social relations is placed under the rule of equal justice, and when human beings learn to cultivate their strongest sympathy with an equal in rights and in cultivation. (John Stuart Mill, *The Subjection of Women*)

The history of men's opposition to women's emancipation is more interesting perhaps than the history of that emancipation itself. (Virginia Woolf, *A Room of One's Own*)

When he was fourteen, Tennyson composed his first marriage poem, *The Devil and the Lady*, an irreverent comedy in Shakespearean blank verse about a wife's suspected adultery. The subject he was so easily to write about at fourteen, became, however, throughout his remaining sixty-odd years, one of increasingly dark and painful concern, a source of disillusionment and a most potent symbol of the growth of generalized corruption and spiritual decay.

The inability to achieve a good marriage in Tennyson's

poetry is the result either of hostile circumstances which prevent a potentially ideal marriage from taking place, or of a failure of trust and love in one or both of the partners once a marriage has taken place. There is a chronological correspondence between the two types of failure: generally speaking, the circumstantial sacrifice of marriage belongs to Tennyson's poems up to and including *Maud*; failure within marriage belongs to the later period, particularly to *Idylls of the King*, the writing of which spans more than twenty years of Tennyson's later career. This second kind of failure invariably has to do with sexual possession: the unfaithful wife, either adulterous or simply lacking in faith like Annie in 'Enoch Arden', or, less frequently, the jealous husband are both cause and symptom of the tragic course of events. The frailty and treachery of the sexual bond become the focus for a generally darkening view of marriage and a metaphor for society's other discontents.

Yet there is no doubt that throughout Tennyson's poetry marriage is thought of as potentially the main source of personal happiness and fulfilment and also as a central, stabilizing social institution. When Arthur asks:

> What happiness to reign a lonely king,
> Vext—O ye stars that shudder over me,
> O earth that soundest hollow under me,
> Vext with waste dreams?
> ('The Coming of Arthur', 81–4)

he echoes the hero of *Maud* who found in the contemplation of a fixed and marriageable love 'the one bright thing to save / My yet young life in the wilds of Time', 'the countercharm of space and hollow sky' (I.556–7, 641). And this repeats what the hero of *The Princess* discovered through love: 'my doubts are dead, / My haunting sense of hollow shows' (VII.327–8), which in its turn echoes the speaker of the early 'The Miller's Daughter': 'ere I saw your eyes, my love, / I had no motion of my own' (43–4). All these male figures conceive of marriage as salvation not merely from loneliness and lack of purpose but also from an existential experience of nothingness, a hollowness at the heart of nature, knowledge and identity. Marriage is the counterforce to despair and death; the vision of a man, wife and child on their way to church is what saves the speaker of 'The Two Voices' from suicide: 'These three made unity so sweet, / My frozen heart began to beat' (421+2). And the epithalamium at the end of *In Memoriam* epitomizes the triumph of life over death the poem has struggled towards:

> Now waiting to be made a wife,
>   Her feet, my darling, on the dead;
>   Their pensive tablets round her head,
> And the most living words of life
>
> Breathed in her ear.
>   (*In Memoriam*, Epil. 49–53)

Such an exalted notion of marriage and the subsequent disillusionment has no obvious correlation with the marriages in Tennyson's life. He experienced his parents' disastrous marriage during his more idealistic youth and grew embittered and misogynist during his own sensible and affectionate union with Emily Sellwood. It is rather the case that Tennyson was a sensitive register of changing attitudes in the nineteenth century towards marriage and also, inextricably linked, towards women. As Jane Rendall has pointed out, the religious revivalism of the late eighteenth and early nineteenth centuries profoundly affected the conception and estimation of marriage. A new 'religion of the Heart' emphasized qualities of obedience, humility, self-denial and purity and introduced a theology 'no longer arid or rational, but relevant to the emotional life of home and family' (Rendall 1985; p. 73). Marriage, at least for the middle classes, ceased to be primarily a working partnership based on economic and class considerations and came to be viewed as a source of moral security and emotional companionship. Such raised expectations of the value of marriage inevitably brought a new value to the position of women, 'exalting what were seen as their essential qualities, defining their own sphere more clearly, offering a limited but positive role within the [Evangelical] movement itself'. As Rendall says, politically the movement was conservative as far as women were concerned because it stressed their limited and adjutant position and their legal inferiority, but because it also elevated their sphere of marriage, within which it offered them the power of influence, its effects were liberalizing, encouraging women in self-realization and social responsibility. The ambiguities of women's position within the Evangelical movement in the early years of the century are well captured in the figure of Dinah Morris in *Adam Bede* (1859); essentially womanly in her purity, self-denial and kindliness, she nevertheless ranges the countryside preaching publicly, although she gives this up in obedience to the wishes of the conservative, 'orthodox' Adam. Dinah's prime function in the novel is as an agent of redemption through her utterances, both private and public, in which she becomes, almost literally, 'the medium of our intercourse with the heavenly world [and] the faithful repositor[y] of the religious principle for the benefit of the present and of the rising generation' (William Wilberforce, quoted Rendall 1985; p. 75).

Adam Bede is set at the turn of the century and pointedly marks the imminent rise into bourgeois respectability of a virtuous working-class man. His candidature for respectability lies in his honest and manly industry and his sense of responsibility but also, particularly, in the high reverence he has for female purity and goodness and his responsiveness to female guidance; his reward lies in his good marriage to Dinah at the end of the novel. In this George Eliot accurately indicates the importance of an ideal marriage as a factor, perhaps the major factor, in the establishment of middle-class hegemony. As Jeffrey Weeks says:

> During the first half of the nineteenth century the domestic ideal and its attendant images became a vital organizing factor in the development of middle-classness, and in the creation of a differentiated class identity. It became, indeed, an expression of class confidence, both against the immoral aristocracy, and against the masses. . . . The norms of domestic life it set forth

drew a clear ideological boundery between rational members of
society and the feckless. (Weeks 1981; p. 28)

The importance of the wife in this elevated concept of
marriage, her training and responsibilities, became a matter
of considerable concern. The whole thrust of even the radical
Mary Wollstonecraft's *A Vindication of the Rights of Women*
(1792) was 'to render [women] truly useful members of
society' by educating them to be the companions rather than
the sexual slaves of men and so raising the moral tone of
marriage and of the whole of society. In Hannah More's
highly successful *Coelebs in Search of a Wife* (1809) the
lineaments of the perfect Victorian wife were foreshadowed;
she must be pious, charitable, sensible, well-informed,
elegant, and with a particular talent for 'rational, animated
conversation' to render her Coelebs's social companion and
moral guardian. By the time Tennyson went to Cambridge
in 1827 the notion of the 'Queen of marriage, a most perfect
wife' was becoming an important focus for middle-class
aspirations to virtue. This attitude towards women was
endorsed for Tennyson by Arthur Hallam whose poems and
essays expounded a religion of love in which the divine, or
at least the privileged, role of woman was prominent:
'Woman's Love was sent / To heal man's tainted heart, and
chasten him for Heaven':

> ... is not Woman worthy to awake
> Our primal thoughts of innocence, and share
>   With us that Wisdom ... communing
>   With Faith, and Hope, and godliest Charity.
>   ('Farewell to the South', 538–46)

This heightened concept of the role of women did not, of
course, extend to rights of self-determination. The value of
women's 'goodness' was in its benefit to men and to the future
of the race: 'If she be small, slight-natured, miserable, / How
shall men grow?' (*The Princess* VII.249–50). When Harriet
Taylor asked in 1851 'why the existence of one-half the
species should be merely ancillary to that of the other—why
each woman should be a mere appendage to a man' (Taylor

1851; p. 301), she was questioning assumptions that few individuals, even those who ardently supported the women's cause, had doubted. Shelley in *The Revolt of Islam* (1818) had framed the debate in terms which were to dominate emancipationist thinking during the rest of the century:

> 'Can man be free if woman be a slave? ...
> 'Can they whose mates are beasts ...
>   ...
>   dare
> To trample their oppressors? in their home
>   Among their babes, thou knowest a curse would wear
> The shape of woman—,
>
>   (II.xliii)

The 'fat-faced curate' in Tennyson's 'Edwin Morris' (written in 1839, at the time when Tennyson was discussing the 'woman question' with Emily Sellwood (Tennyson 1897; I.248)) crudely restates this position when he says, 'I take it, God made the woman for the man, / And for the good and increase of the world.' During the marriage debate during the years that follow, the problem will be to preserve the terms of this power relation between men and women whilst ennobling and idealizing women. As John Killham has amply demonstrated, Tennyson was exposed to this debate through his membership at Cambridge of the Apostles, the group of idealistic undergraduates amongst whom the 'feminist' writings of William Thompson, F.D. Maurice and Charles Buller circulated. These provided the ideas which were to inform Tennyson's own contribution to the debate, *The Princess* (1847).

The Princess was one of a group of writings published in the middle of the century which expressed a confidence in the ability of marriage to transcend its bare legal requirements by giving flesh to its sacramental potential whilst at the same time providing qualities of emotional and intellectual partnership between two equal if complementary individuals: in fact, the companionate marriage which is idealistically celebrated at the end of *Jane Eyre* (1847):

I am my husband's life as fully as he is mine . . . we are ever
together. . . . We talk, I believe, all day long: to talk to each
other is but a more animated and an audible thinking . . . we are
precisely suited in character—perfect concord is the result.

The group of writings to which *The Princess* and *Jane Eyre*
belong includes A.H. Clough's *The Bothie of Tober-na-
Vuolich* (1848), Elizabeth Gaskell's *North and South* (1855),
Coventry Patmore's *The Angel in the House* (1854–60), and
Elizabeth Barrett's *Aurora Leigh* (1857). In their various
ways, these works summarize the debates of the preceding
years on marriage and the position of women. For the most
part, they are characterized by heroines of unusual intellectual and moral independence whose capitulation into
marriage is from a position of strength and whose marriages
promise to become the kind Jane Eyre and Rochester
achieve. The exceptions to this are Patmore's poem and, to a
lesser extent, Clough's, in which the women are socially and
intellectually, but not spiritually, inferior. In Patmore's
poem, particularly, the emphasis is on marriage as a
sacrament and in this respect the poem is saved from some of
the doubts encountered in the other works in which a greater
secularism forces the debate into consideration of the social
and sexual roles appropriate to each partner in this changed
concept of marriage. Of all these works, *The Princess* is the
most comprehensive in its range of discussion of the women-
and-marriage question; it is also the most anxious. The
others show interest, doubt, optimism, failure of nerve,
euphoria; *The Princess* also exhibits these attitudes, but
additionally it is an expression of acute anxiety concerning
male sexual needs and definitions. On the level of its surface
argument the poem carefully and not unsympathetically
states women's educational demands and appears to effect a
liberal compromise between these demands and the requirements of marriage and maternity. But as Kate Millett has
pointed out, the poem takes fright at its own daring and turns
away from the logical pursuit of its argument to plead with
'urgent insecurity' the fear that if women become indepen-
dent they may cease to love men and bear their children, may

no longer succour and console them, no longer serve, as
Virginia Woolf has expressed it, as

> looking glasses possessing the magic and delicious power of
> reflecting the figure of man at twice its natural size. [This]
> looking glass is of supreme importance because it charges the
> vitality; it stimulates the nervous system. Take it away and man
> may die. (Woolf 1945; pp. 37–8)

The Princess is about saving man from death, from the death
of his manhood in literal sexual terms, and also from the
death of his function, powers and self-image as a man. It is a
strategy for survival. To save himself from death, the
nameless Prince-hero of the poem, all men and Everyman, is
prepared to use the ancient weapons of coercion and violence
to protect himself, but he also employs some new ones—
new, at least, in men's declaration of their tactics—and they
are those of sentimentality, weakness and dependency. In
this he is prepared to change, and, within limits, to redefine
his masculinity; he will become a new man in order to protect
an old system.

Kate Millett says that the Prince is 'really his father's boy',
and that his father is 'a male supremacist of the most vulgar
and abusive variety' (Millett 1972; pp. 78–9). Whilst it is
true that both men overcome and control the women they
want, the Prince's style is very different from his father's and
he uses tactics the old king would have scorned. His courting
was of the muscular, militaristic type: '[He] leaps in / Among
the women, snares them by the score / Flattered and
flustered, wins, though dashed with death / He reddens what
he kisses' (V.155–8). This is a style echoed by the Prince's
friend Cyril, whose desire for Lady Psyche is a similarly
uncomplicated mixture of lust and acquisitiveness—'For
dear are those three castles to my wants, / And dear is Lady
Psyche to my heart' (II. 395–6)—and who when drunk lays
bare the crudeness of his sexual needs in bawdy songs
(IV.137–41). But these are the men of yesterday, and
although they will survive well enough amongst the 'soft and
milky rabble of womankind' (VI.290), they are no match for
the new woman.

The Prince, by contrast, is effeminate, 'with lengths of yellow ringlet, like a girl' (I.3), he dislikes violence—'loth by brainless war / To cleave the rift of difference deeper yet' (V.290–1)—although he will use it if necessary, and he doesn't mind being made a fool of, by dressing as a 'draggled mawkin', to gain his ends. He professes sympathy for the woman's cause—'not a scorner of your sex / But venerator, zealous it should be / All that it might be' (IV.402–4)—and he is not daunted by Ida's height and presence, nor by her imperiousness and learning which actually excite him to 'blissful palpitations in the blood'. He is also a romantic idealist, one of Tennyson's lovers whose twinning with their other selves occurred at birth and who has persisted in narcissistic identification with his love object:

> when a boy, you stooped to me
> From all high places, lived in all fair lights,
> Came in long breezes rapt from inmost south
> And blown to inmost north; at eve and dawn
> With Ida, Ida, Ida, rang the woods;
> (IV.409–13)

Most effective in his courting, however, is his need for Ida which he is not ashamed to expose and exploit—'Yea, let her see me fall!'—and his use of weakness to secure what strength could not: 'I shall die tonight. / Stoop down and seem to kiss me ere I die' (VII.134–5). (This is an aspect of the Prince which Tennyson intensified in his introduction, in the fourth edition of the poem, of the 'wierd seizures' that afflict the Prince and which his union with Ida dispels: 'My doubts are dead, / My haunting sense of hollow shows: the change / This truthful change in thee has killed it' (VII.327–9).) The role he plays is a mixture of Woody Allen-type jester and insatiable child who demands to be born into his masculine heritage through the possession of the woman's body and voice. What is enacted is a perverse creation story: the woman gives him life—'breathe[s] upon my brows'—but it is a Frankenstein birth because the creature then becomes the one who controls the creator, directs her actions and speaks on her behalf:

'Look up, and let thy nature strike on mine,
Like yonder morning on the blind half-world;
Approach and fear not; breathe upon my brows; ...
Accomplish thou my manhood and thyself;
Lay thy sweet hands in mine and trust to me.'
(VII.330–45)

To all this Princess Ida opposes a progressive and, in nineteenth-century terms, a modern outlook. She is interested in science, has trained in medicine and geology, she is industrious, efficient and well-organized and she is a social reformer. Although a poet, she has no sympathy with poetry 'such as moans about the retrospect' or which 'haunt[s] ... the mouldered lodges of the past' (IV.67,44–5) but prefers rather to write of 'freedom, force and growth / Of spirit than [of] junketing and love' (IV.123–4) and in general has a low regard for romantic love, recognizing it as men 'playing the slave to gain the tyranny.' Her feminist arguments are ones John Stuart Mill would be ready to use in another twenty years and her rationality such as T.H. Huxley could have commended. In many respects she is the very spirit of Victorian liberal enlightenment and certainly she is a better man than the Prince. This, of course, is just the problem. The implications of her superiority are serious for they expose a dangerous contradiction within the marriage debate: an exalted notion of marriage requires that the female partner shall be educated and self-determining, 'living wills, and sphered / Whole in ourselves and owed to none' (IV.129–30), as Ida puts it, and certainly not the 'higher domestic servant' J.S. Mill regretted his mother had been. Yet the presence, or the promise, of this new 'manly' woman poses a threat not just to the marriage relationship, but also to the male self-image which previously had found its definition in the magnifying looking-glass properties of acknowledged female weakness.

Tennyson's solution to the dilemma is to alter the terms of the argument. Ida's superiority, her claims for educational opportunity for women, and her outrage at the intrusion of 'a rout of saucy boys ... would-be quenchers of the light to be',

are swept aside in the emotionalism of battle, and the
rationality of her university is replaced by the subjectivity of
domestic politics in which the college is converted to a
hospital and the women to nurse-mothers to the men, and
Ida's 'iron will [is] broken'. Tennyson is sufficiently embarrassed by this sleight of hand to cause the modern-day
Walter to say, 'I wish she had not yielded' (Concl. 5), but of
course the inference is that if she had not there would have
been no love and marriage, no peaceful ending, nothing but
chaos and war. When the argument on women's rights re-
sumes Ida's superiority is not denied, merely tamed and
contained within a new philosophy of marriage as complementarity which the Prince, loquacious in victory, expounds:

> '. . . in true marriage lies
> Nor equal, nor unequal: each fulfils
> Defect in each, and always thought in thought,
> Purpose in purpose, will in will, they grow,
> The single pure and perfect animal,
> The two-celled heart beating, with one full stroke,
> Life.'
>
> (VII.284–9)

It becomes obvious that the model for Tennyson's ideal
marriage is biological, based on a radical and pervasive
notion of a natural sexual difference which inevitably
contains within it the definitions of 'distinctive womanhood'
which were to thwart the development of the women's
movement throughout the nineteenth century and beyond.
The Princess seems to be engaged upon a question J.S. Mill
was to pose twenty years later in *The Subjection of Women*
(1869): why, Mill asks, if it is natural for women to become
wives and mothers, does society compel them to do so by
offering them no alternative means of existence? It might be
supposed, Mill continues, from the present constitution of
society 'that the alleged natural vocation of women was of all
things the most repugnant to their nature. . . . If this is the
real opinion of men in general, it would be well that it should
be spoken out' (Mill 1970; p. 244). Such an opinion is
'spoken out' in *The Princess* in as much as Ida represents that

feared repugnance: 'Yet will we say for children, would they grew / Like field-flowers everywhere!' (III.234–5), she says, heretically. But as the poem illustrates, 'the present constitution of society' in 1847, as much as in the medieval period the poem is set in, imposes a two-fold repression upon the exercise of such repugnance: the physical violence the Prince's father recommends and the ideological pressure the prince himself brings to bear.

Ida's defeat is her reclamation into an unredeemed, unaltered marriage relationship; the marriage overall may be more courteous and dignified, one of 'the world's great bridals, chaste and calm', but Ida's relationship to the Prince adheres to a power structure no different from that adhered to by his parents'. This is strikingly signalled in the question of who controls language; from being a speaker, Ida becomes a listener, from being a poet she becomes the reader of other (men's) poetry. Like her modern counterpart, Lilia, she becomes the accompaniment to the words of men: 'the women sang / Between the rougher voices of the men, / Like linnets in the pauses of the wind' (Prol. 236–8) is how Lilia's contribution to the medley is described, and this becomes the Prince's prescription for Ida's role in marriage: 'Like perfect music unto noble words' (VII. 270). Ida's eventual silence, passivity and self-doubt are dressed out in the blushings, pallor, sighs, mild eyes and trembling voice which are the conventional attributes of virtuous womanhood. Her submission is sealed in the moment of sexual surrender when the Prince can banish the recalcitrant 'falser self' which her independence has created and remake her as 'woman', Aphrodite, erotic image and sexual property. The transfer of power is described in a variation of another creation myth, that of Orpheus and Eurydice:

> ... mute she glided forth,
> Nor glanced behind her, and I sank and slept,
> Filled through and through with Love, a happy sleep.
> (VII.155–7)

Speechless and unseeing, drained of her power, Ida delivers
the Prince from death into life and love more successfully
and more obediently than Orpheus could his Eurydice.

In some r spects, *The Princess* seems to achieve what *The
Lover's Tale* could not, that is, successfully to combine a
story of romantic love, about a Prince and Princess who are
pledged from 'the flaxen curl to the gray lock' in a life of
passionate union, with the strenuously argued transaction of
their marriage. But in this combining process, the com-
ponent of romantic love is curiously distanced and ancillary.
Critics from Harold Nicolson to Kate Millett have com-
mented on the luminous quality of the songs in *The Princess*
as contrasted with the rather prosaic blank verse of the
narrative. But this is just the point: the poem is earnestly
concerned to hammer out the conditions of modern marriage
whilst at the same time adorning and idealizing it (one could
say *palliating* it) with romantic, narcissistic notions of love.
The divisive nature of this is recognized, although for
different purposes, by both the Prince and Ida. 'I bear ... a
life / Less mine than yours ... I babbled for you, as babies for
the moon', says the Prince, declaring his romantic creden-
tials, but *now*, 'those winters of abeyance all worn out, / A
man I came to see you' (IV.404–8, 420–1), and it is now that
the serious, manly and unromantic business of matrimonial
coercion must begin. Ida likewise dismisses romantic love as
weakness, interestingly enough weakness of a feminine kind:
'Poor boy,' she says on hearing of the Prince's lovesickness,
'... to nurse a blind ideal like a girl, / Methinks he seems no
better than a girl' (III.198–202). This division is presaged in
the prologue, where the men decide to tell the story and the
women to supply the songs, and it is developed in the
relegation of romantic love to lyrics within the poem, all of
which (if one allows the Prince's falsetto contribution of 'O
Swallow, Swallow') are sung by women. The implication is
that love is to do with ideality, and not with the practical and
social world, and moreover that the subjective mode of
expressing that ideality, lyric poetry, likewise belongs to a
marginalized and feminine voice. 'In any man who utters the
other's absence', says Roland Barthes, '*something feminine* is

declared: this man who waits and who suffers from his waiting is miraculously feminized. A man is not feminized because he is inverted but because he is in love' (Barthes 1979; p. 14). The Prince's effeminacy is the correlative of his lovesick state which finds appropriate expression in the songs of the women, including the poems that Ida reads after she has been reclaimed into femininity. With the success of his courtship, which signals his progress from the narcissistic world of romantic love into the interpersonal world of marriage, the Prince accomplishes his manhood and assumes the narrative and didactic authority that characterizes the conclusion of this part of the poem. But, as Chapter 4 of this study will show in relation to *In Memoriam*, Tennyson will return to the use of a feminized utterance in writing where it is most appropriate, in elegy, the poetry of love and absence.

By 1855, eight years after *The Princess* Tennyson had planned his longest marriage poem, *Idylls of the King*. He published four (of an eventual twelve) parts of this in 1859; 'Enid', 'Vivien', 'Elaine', 'Guinevere'. He had been fascinated by the Arthurian story for many years but his earlier attempts suggest that he had originally been less interested in its sexual elements than he was in 1859 where these are the dominant concern. The 1859 group of poems present two contrasting pairs of virtuous and fallen women who represent a good and a bad wife and their unmarried counterparts. Enid is the child of loving, noble parents, is sweet-voiced as a bird and is a 'blossom vermeil-white'; she is modest and obedient and her husband Geraint is assured of her love: 'I felt / That I could rest, a rock in ebbs and flows, / Fixt on her faith' ('The Marriage of Geraint', 811–13*). Vivien is an orphan of rebels against the king ('born from death was I / Among the dead and sown upon the wind' ('Merlin and Vivien', 44–5)), and she is impure and deceitful, and Merlin is 'overtalked and overworn' and finally

---

* 'Enid' was expanded to 'Geraint and Enid' in 1870, divided into two parts in 1873 and given the final titles of 'The Marriage of Geraint' and 'Geraint and Enid' in 1886.

entrapped by her, 'lost to life and use and name and fame' (212). Both women follow their men into the wilderness, but Enid's journey is at the behest of her husband whereas Vivien's is an act of defiance, done against Merlin's wishes. Significantly, Enid is silent except where her husband's life is in danger; Vivien, by contrast, is loquacious and theatrical, an accomplished manipulator. Together they provide the harlot and good wife figures in the sexual scenario. They are complemented by Elaine and Guinevere as pure virgin and remorseful adulteress. The world of the *Idylls* is highly schematic and the four women present what we now think of as Victorian stereotypes of womanhood.

The iconographic landscape of the *Idylls* has encouraged critics of the poem, following Tennyson himself, to interpret the sexual relations symbolically, or parabolically, as Tennyson liked to say, and to ignore their literal significance. And, of course, the *Idylls* are not 'realistic' in the same way as *The Princess* which is, as John Killham has said, 'a little novel . . . in verse' (Killham 1958; p. 1).

Nevertheless, interpretations which dwell on the 'abstract' nature of the *Idylls* have tended to obscure the fact that they are very much about marriage and represent a hardening of attitudes towards it. Marriage in the *Idylls* is not a social institution to be debated and possibly modified according to the changing needs of society, as it had been to some extent in *The Princess*, but an alliance within fixed boundaries of rigidly defined moral and aesthetic absolutes. For Tennyson, the debate about marriage has ended; his concern now is with the fulfilling of its exacting and immutable conditions. Having explored the nature of marriage in *The Princess*, and having arrived, so it must have seemed, at a 'new', exalted conception of this 'chaste and pure' union, there follows in the *Idylls* of 1859 a scrutiny of the perils which beset marriage: uxoriousness, prostitution, adultery, sterility.

'Enid' portrays the only satisfactory marriage in the *Idylls* and the only one in which there are living children. But this happy conclusion is described perfunctorily (963–7) and the weight of the poem lies instead in a cautionary prescription of the conditions necessary to such a conclusion. Geraint's situation in marriage is an interesting development from *The Princess* in that he is the doting and idealistic husband the Prince might well have become and in his cultivation of the domestic and tender virtues he seems to be following the Prince's injunction: 'Yet in the long years liker must they grow; / The man be more of woman, she of man' (VII.263–4). But the problem with a heightened personal life like this is that it leads to neglect of public duties and to an erosion of Geraint's manhood which hitherto has been defined by knightly conduct in a sphere quite separate from Enid's. He has become effeminate, 'a prince whose manhood was all gone, / And molten down in mere uxoriousness' ('The Marriage of Geraint', 59–60). To correct the effeminacy requires, of course, violent combat on the part of the man and, equally important, a wife who is unquestioningly devoted, a patient Griselda to provide the magnifying mirror for his masculine authority. The story ends with Enid, 'the Fair', 'the Good', as nurse and mother and Geraint as 'foremost in the chase, / And victor at the tilt and tournament . . . and man of men' ('Geraint and Enid', 958–60), attributes which are reminiscent of the recipe for marital success recommended by the old king in *The Princess*. The difference in the marriage roles has been reinstated and emphasized; not 'liker' have they grown but 'diverse'. In this story Tennyson has dramatized an anxiety implicit in the conclusion to *The Princess*; intensity, intimacy and identity of interests between the marriage partners, qualities prominent in the optimistic, mid-century conceptions of the companionate marriage, may, Tennyson suggests in 'Enid', entail loss of function, status and identity, for the man primarily, but to some extent for the woman too. The argument becomes a Möbius strip of irresolution: marriage must be reformed along egalitarian lines but such would destroy the conditions which constitute the fundamental conception of marriage in patriarchal society. In Tennyson's increasing concern to preserve difference, perceived optimistically as complementarity in the less intransigent *The Princess*, but openly acknowledged as opposition in 'Enid', lies a recognition that sexual difference teaches us the road to

differences of all other kinds—class, race, group—and that
therefore to change the structure of marriage is to undermine
the structures of society. Geraint's manhood is accomplished
by Enid's obedience to his authority and by her sense of his
status—'I cannot love my lord and not his name' ('The
Marriage of Geraint', 92)—, and this includes his ability to
rule: 'And there he kept the justice of the King / So
vigorously yet mildly' ('Geraint and Enid', 955–6). Previously his uxoriousness had made him 'Forgetful of his
princedom and its cares' but now, strengthened in the proof
of his husbandly authority, he is a model of the enlightened
Victorian colonialist or captain of industry.

In 'Enid' the adultery of Guinevere is held partly responsible for what goes wrong, and throughout the rest of the
Idylls she is increasingly blamed for the sins committed by
the knights of Camelot against their social order: fratricide,
suicide, murder, religious excess, rebellion, unchastity, and
further adultery. This is Tennyson's own emphasis; in his
main source, Malory's *Le Morte Darthur*, the adultery of
Guinevere and Lancelot is important but it is not the main
cause Tennyson makes it. Gerhard Joseph says: 'The mind
may boggle at the Victorian conception of a single woman's
power for good or ill, but we are supposed to take with
complete seriousness Arthur's accusation . . . that the "loath-
some opposite" of "all" he desired came about "all through"
his false queen' (Joseph 1969; p. 173). But the conception is
not at all mind-boggling if one sees in Victorian marriage the
very pivot and paradigm of middle-class power relations
throughout society. The obedience and faithfulness of a
wife, and the ability of a husband to exact these conditions
from her, were not simply a question of ensuring legitimacy
of inheritance; they provided the necessary psychological
basis for successful control of the 'heathen hordes'. The
trappings of courtly love and medieval chivalry cannot hide
and perhaps even emphasize the connection Tennyson
makes between the external power relations of class control
of wealth, labour and status, and the internal sexual politics
of courtship, marriage and sexual difference. The insurrec-
tionist Red Knight, whose message to Arthur is that 'his hour

is come, / The heathen are upon him, his long lance / Broken, and his Excalibur a straw' ('The Last Tournament', 86–8), rightly equates this public anarchy with the sexual anarchy of Arthur's court which the Red Knight's Round table in the North grotesquely reflects.

Gerhard Joseph points out that the stress on Guinevere's culpability is coupled with the gradual extenuation of Lancelot. Guinevere's prime responsibility is first made clear in a conversation between her and Lancelot in 'Balin and Balan' in which her carnality—' "Sweeter to me" she said "this garden rose / Deep-hued and many-folded!"' (264–5)—is blamed for Lancelot's trance-like enslavement. In the final sequence of the *Idylls*, 'Balin and Balan' is placed fourth in the Round Table books, coming after the relatively happy 'Gareth and Lynette' and the two Enid books. Yet 'Balin and Balan' was the last book to be published (1885) and its insertion into the final scheme at this late stage indicates Tennyson's intention to clarify a moral always inherent in his conception of the Arthurian legends: not only that marriage is the hub of society but that when this centre will not hold, it is women who are to blame. Men are destroyed by women in the *Idylls*: Arthur and Lancelot, Balin and Balan by Guinevere, Merlin by Vivien, Pelleas by Ettarre; even the dutiful, chaste Enid causes a perilous instability in Geraint, and the 'delicately pure and marvellously fair' Elaine, whose 'love is beyond all love / In women', brings to Lancelot not solace but despair and 'remorseful pain'. Of all these victims of women's power, Pelleas is the most extreme example of a man reduced to lawlessness by a woman. His is a story anticipated in the conduct of the heroes of both *The Princess* and *Maud* who resort to violence to enforce or replace the love of women. Pelleas's transformation into the Red Knight after the thwarting of his love for Ettarre is Tennyson's transformation of the pragmatic solution to this problem in Malory (where Pelleas finds happiness with the Lady of the Lake) to a warning so dire as to constitute blackmail: if women will not give men the love they want, then havoc will result, not merely the 'heathen hordes' of external rebellion but the discharge of the sexual energies of men in violence.

Implicit in the *Idylls* is the assumption of a given and natural force of male sexuality of an explosive quality; if this cannot be safely defused by the right kind of woman then it will blow up with the random destructiveness of the Red Knight's killing of 'whatever knight' happens to cross his path. As William Acton, writing in 1857, put it:

> Gunpowder remains harmless till the spark falls upon it; the match, until struck, retains the hidden fire, so lust remains dormant till called into being . . . intercourse with a depraved woman debases the mind, and gradually hardens the heart . . . (Acton 1968; p. 119)

In Tennyson's poem, Tristram, *l'homme moyen sensuel*, 'worldling of the world', is spokesman for this determinist view of male sexuality:

> For feel this arm of mine—the tide within
> Red with free chase and heather-scented air,
> Pulsing full man; can Arthur make me pure
> As any maiden child? . . .
> . . . we are not angels here
> Nor shall be:
>   ('The Last Tournament', 685–94)

The responsibility women bear for the safe conduct of men through this world of perilous natural forces is not only total but wellnigh impossible to discharge. The strict requirements for success are established early in the *Idylls* in the depiction of Enid's courtship and marriage. Enid is virtuous and devoted but she must be tested to prove that she is so beyond all doubt. In Enid's story the success of marriage is measured in terms of a woman's ideal conduct, just as in subsequent stories marriage is imperilled by womanly conduct less perfect than hers. Tennyson has travelled a long way in his views on marriage from 'The Miller's Daughter' to *Idylls of the King*; an early idealism in which the hope of marriage was that it might be the natural and spontaneous outcome of youthful love has been replaced by a sense that it is an institution of such exacting and inexorable conditions that it is doomed to failure.

   This shift in attitude is accompanied by a change in the
nature of Tennyson's writing from the poetry of stasis to that
of narrative. In romantic love, in the enthralment of the
narcissistic moment which cannot move beyond itself, the
writing is suspenseful, self-regarding, inert, and with an
effect of intoxification that Edward Fitzgerald noted as 'the
old champagne flavour' of Tennyson's early verse. The terms
of this discourse of romantic love are set out in *The Lover's
Tale*:

                          the sunshine seemed to brood
        More warmly on the heart than on the brow.
        We often paused, and, looking back, we saw
        The clefts and openings in the mountains filled
        With the blue valley and the glistening brooks,
        And all the low dark groves, a land of love!
        A land of promise, a land of memory,
        A land of promise flowing with the milk
        And honey of delicious memories!
        And down to sea, and far as eye could ken,
        Each way from verge to verge a Holy Land,
        Still growing holier as you neared the bay,
        For there the Temple stood.
                                          (I.320–32)

A land of love indeed, for the mild sublimity of this
passage—the cleft and mountain, blue valley and glistening
brooks—conjures a landscape looked back upon as to a
'maternal . . . poultice—a reassuring balm' in a yearning for
an unreachable holy land where promise and memory forever
cancel each other out. This is the landscape of Tennyson's
most brilliant early work—'a fantasma of beauty. . . . You
can no more touch or clasp it, than beauty in a dream. It is
not less beautiful, for *that*; but less sensual it *is*' (Barrett
1954; p. 152)—which invokes a world of sleep and enchant-
ment, of the halted gesture, the unheard speech, the uncon-
summated desire; of something always about to happen:
what Christopher Ricks calls the 'art of the penultimate':

        Dreaming, she knew it was a dream:
        She felt he was and was not there.

> She woke: the babble of the stream
>   Fell, and, without, the steady glare
> Shrank one sick willow sere and small.
>   The river-bed was dusty-white;
>   And all the furnace of the light
> Struck up against the blinding wall.
>   She whispered, with a stifled moan
>   More inward than at night or morn,
>   'Sweet Mother, let me not here alone
>   Live forgotten and die forlorn.'
>   ('Mariana in the South', 49–60)

Although this kind of writing persists into Tennyson's later poetry ('Tears, idle tears' and 'Now sleeps the crimson petal' in *The Princess*, for example, and a passage such as 'The slender acacia would not shake / One long milk-bloom on the tree' in *Maud* (I.894–901)), it is progressively overridden by the linearity and purposefulness of narrative, culminating in the relentless and repetitive (telling the story again and again) proceeding of *Idylls of the King*. Although there are powerful delineations of guilt, shame, need, fear and bewilderment in this long marriage poem of Tennyson's maturity, there are no descriptions of the type just quoted. When Tennyson writes of marriage, which inevitably involves notions of progression, futurity and social organization, this requires not the 'enchanted moan' (*Maud* I.660) of love poetry but the sequential purpose of story-telling. But as Tennyson's narrative of marriage unfolds, it comes clear that not only is there is such thing as *married love* (according to the conceptions Tennyson has used this becomes an oxymoronic absurdity) but also that the story of marriage taken merely as a social arrangement comes to represent a doomed enterprise, that sexual relations founder on the gender constructs which characterize them. That Tennyson became so pessimistic in the thirty or so years that separated 'The Miller's Daughter' and *Idylls of the King* is due to the development of his understanding of what constitutes the nature of man and, more particularly, the nature of woman.

SECTION B: MEN

CHAPTER THREE

Strong Men and the Contours
of Manliness

'I didn't roar out a bit, you know,' Tom said. . . . 'It's cowardly to
roar.'

But Maggie would have it that when anything hurt you very
much, it was quite permissible to cry out . . . (George Eliot, *The
Mill on the Floss*).

'You are thinking,' he said, 'that my face is old and tired. You are
thinking that I talk of power, and yet I am not able even to
prevent the decay of my own body. Can you not understand,
Winston, that the individual is only a cell? The weariness of the
cell is the vigour of the organism. Do you die when you cut your
fingernails?' (George Orwell, *Nineteen Eighty-Four*).

In describing the 'masculine reticence as to the tender
emotions' which Tom Tulliver, even as a very youthful 'pink
and white bit of masculinity', must display if he is to sustain
his role as only son and elder brother, George Eliot was
drawing on definitions of manliness which by 1860, the date
of *The Mill on the Floss*, had been developed and codified
with a self-conscious thoroughness that gave them, at least
among the middle classes, gospel status.

'Manliness' and 'masculinity' were by no means identical
concepts although they obviously overlapped. 'Masculinity'
described a set of beliefs about male sexuality which were, as
Jeffrey Weeks has pointed out, 'inextricably linked to
concepts of male self-expression and power' (Weeks 1981;

p. 39). 'Manliness', however, was not merely a question of sexual performance. Virility, as William Acton had noted in 1857, may be essential 'to give a man that consciousness of his dignity, of his character as head and ruler, and of his importance' (quoted in Weeks, ibid.), but as Acton's comment implies, virility had to be consciously translated into social behaviour recognizably manly.

The translation involved a contradiction: the socially acceptable behaviour denoting manliness—being a strong, reliable worker, an authoritative yet loving husband and father, and a respected public figure—may have been nourished by a man's consciousness of his masculinity but it also disallowed all but the most severely regulated display of that masculinity. Manliness therefore came to mean the exercise of restraint upon the manifestations of male sexuality—the passion, lust, aggression, violence and neediness of the 'pulsing full man' of Tristram's description—and either their suppression or their redirection into sanctioned forms. The extent of a man's mastery and redirection of powerful sexual energies became a measure of the manliness of his character. 'Manliness' implied virility but expressed itself in social terms as courage, capacity for toil, protectiveness towards the weak, self-control and emotional reticence. These qualities were not merely a question of manners but of self-respect and self-definition. As Mr Thornton in *North and South* says, 'when we speak of ... "a man" we consider him not merely with regard to his fellow-men but in relation to himself,—to life—to time—to eternity'.

Several novels of the mid-century besides *North and South* were concerned with the nature of manliness, or its near neighbour, gentlemanliness: *The Tenant of Wildfell Hall* (1848), *John Halifax, Gentleman* (1857) and *Great Expectations* (1861), for instance, all explore definitions of manliness for the benefit of their aspirant bourgeois readership. Of the novels of this kind, *Adam Bede* is the most paradigmatic. Published in the same year (1859) as Tennyson published the first four books of what was to be *Idylls of the King*, *Adam Bede* was provocatively and

tendentiously concerned not only with a male protagonist—
in itself unusual for a woman novelist—but with English
manhood: Adam Bede. The self-consciousness and audacity
of such an undertaking, and the programmatic nature of the
novel itself, proclaim it an interesting authority on the
subject; it both offers and questions definitions concerning
manhood, and its insights reach backwards and forwards
into other Victorian writing, including Tennyson's.

Adam's physical qualities—he is tall, muscular, deep-
voiced, with a 'large and roughly hewn' face—indicate an
indisputable masculinity. The translation of this strength
and virility into manliness shows itself in his reliability as a
worker, his honesty and steadfastness and his sense of his
own importance, that 'consciousness of his dignity, of his
character as head and ruler' that Acton spoke of. The
deficiencies of his character, which the novel is at pains to
expose and ameliorate, derive from this manliness, or at least
are a concomitant of the *repression* of aggression and virility
necessary to the social construction of manliness. Adam is
not spontaneously kind—'idle tramps felt sure they would
get a copper from Seth; they scarcely ever spoke to Adam'—
and he is impatient and intolerant and narrowly practical in
his responses: when he sees a beautiful tree he calculates 'the
height and contents of [its] trunk to a nicety'. But his most
serious failing is a kind of emotional cowardice which makes
him reluctant to confront Hetty's crime and her misery:
'This brave active man . . . trembled at the thought of seeing
her changed face, as a timid woman trembles at the thought
of the surgeon's knife.' Throughout the novel Adam is
abjured to 'bear sorrow manfully', that is, not to make
extravagant or expressive displays of grief or anger, but
instead, as Mr Irwine tells him, to 'think of, and act for'
others: 'I expect it from your strength of mind Adam—from
your sense of duty to God and man—that you will try to act
as long as action can be of any use.' The implication is that, as
a corollary of the mastery of his powerful body and masculine
desires, Adam's emotional life must be similarly disciplined
and discharged into useful channels. The code of manliness
Mr Irwine adumbrates is based on an economy of feeling in

which emotional investment should result in commensurately practical returns. Otherwise, feeling, like unregulated sexuality, would spend itself in profligate and probably destructive wastefulness.

George Eliot makes clear, however, that even in the practical world of Hayslope, action, however important, is not enough. Expressive behaviour—tears, gestures, touches, and above all the speech of emotion—is also necessary, to bring 'relief from what [is] becoming unbearable' and to create a flow of sympathy between human beings. Dinah's communicative skill—her 'unpremeditated eloquence, which opens the inward drama of the speaker's emotions'—releases the prohibition that Adam's manliness has imposed upon him so that he can talk to Hetty and forgive her, and thereby become a better man.

Yet though it is fitting that Adam should display his anguish at times of extreme poignancy, for him to do so often or to do so spontaneously without Dinah's mediation would be evidence of weakness. To cry, to speak wildly or too feelingly are signs of effeminacy, and so too are squeamishness, sentimentality and other instances of lack of self-mastery such as dreaminess and introspection. Seth's relative effeminacy is established early in the novel in his forgetfulness at work and his easy tears over Dinah as well as in his kindliness and his submissiveness to Adam. His lack of masculinity is evident in his appearance in which he is a blurred and indeterminate version of Adam (interestingly, he has the 'coronal arch . . . over the brow' that Tennyson noticed in Arthur Hallam), and he notably lacks sexual passion and possessiveness; happy to love Dinah with a 'venerating love . . . hardly distinguishable from religious feeling' and to find 'earthly happiness' in her and Adam's children, his kind of spontaneous goodness, almost saintliness, precludes masculinity, just as the manliness of Adam precludes the gentle expressiveness of Seth. Together the two men provide an ideal which haunts the novel but which is apparently unrealizable in practice. This ideal is expressed through Dinah's image of Christ in whom are combined active manliness and womanly sympathy and expressiveness: he is 'great and mighty and can do what he will' yet 'he spoke very tenderly to poor sinners'. Likewise, Christ's disciple, Charles Wesley, was strong and hardy yet 'his voice was very soft and beautiful'. This is an ideal of manhood which Tennyson saw foreshadowed in Arthur Hallam and which he figuratively explored in the character of King Arthur in *Idylls of the King*:

> ... manhood fused with female grace
> In such a sort, the child would twine
> A trustful hand, unasked, in thine,
> And find his comfort in thy face;
> (*In Memoriam* CIX,17–20)

The three-way 'marriage' at the end of *Adam Bede*—Adam, Seth and Dinah—is an idyllic containment of the irreconcilables within the categories of sexual difference of the period. As sister to one and wife to the other, now home-centred in her child-rearing role, Dinah unites the separate halves of the ideal whole the brothers represent. Adam and Seth set the terms of a debate about male power, action and responsibility and the relation of these to the consciousness and repression of male sexuality and emotional need. Dinah provides the figure of the female go-between in this scene of arbitration over what constitutes a good man.

* * *

There is a marked scarcity of manly men in Tennyson's poetry. In contrast to Browning's characters, who are unmistakably masculine, Tennyson's male figures are, for the most part, vacillating, weak and effeminate and display a vulnerability which belies the patrician image that Tennyson himself presented, particularly throughout his Laureate years. There are exceptions to this generalization: characters in *Idylls*, such as Gareth and Tristram, Enoch Arden perhaps, and a group of old or ageing men who, by reputation at least, are heroic: Ulysses, Tithonus, Tiresias and the Arthur of 'Morte d'Arthur'. This last group are the

protagonists of poems written in the immediate aftermath of
Arthur Hallam's death. In his grief for Hallam, Tennyson
assumed a 'mask of age' and deflected his sorrow and
bewilderment into heroic or gnomic figures from myth and
legend. But although heroic in gesture, these poems about
old men were in some respects an evasion of a 'proper' manly
role which should surely have been that of a young man
(Tennyson was twenty-four at the time), a David mourning
a Jonathan, a successor to the ever-youthful second generation of Romantic poets Hallam so much admired and, more
important, an inheritor of an elegiac tradition which in
Milton's *Lycidas* and Shelley's *Adonais* had, with most
youthful and manly directness, confronted the enormity of
early death.

In each case, Tennyson's old men poems enact a scene in
which an ageing man finds solace in the contemplation of
death: as a last adventure for Ulysses, as release from
wearying mortality for Tithonus, as noble self-sacrifice for
Tiresias, and as part of a progressive development—'The
old order changeth, yielding place to new'—for Arthur.
Tennyson seems to be rehearsing four ways of dying: the
heroic, the nihilistic, the Christian and the evolutionary. In
each exercise, the old men are placed in a triangular
relationship with a younger man and a woman: Telemachus
and the 'agèd wife' in 'Ulysses', Tithonus's younger self and
Aurora in 'Tithonus', Menœceus and Pallas Athene in
'Tiresias', and Sir Bedevere and the Lady of the Lake in
'Morte d'Arthur'. The younger men are shadowy observers
or companions in the protagonists' journey towards death,
mute commentators on the old men's anguish and mortal
desire. The women are even more shadowy and distant yet
they are all-important points of reference, indeed they *cause*
the action in the poems in that they are the locus of anxiety
and dissatisfaction which generates the move towards death.
Death is proposed as a solution to problems to do with
women which cannot be otherwise solved: the impregna-
bility of the 'agèd wife', Aurora's insatiability, Pallas Athene's
implacability, and the inexorability of the Lady of the
Lake, all these provoke crises not merely of masculinity—

the failure in virility of the protagonists is clear—but of manliness also. The roles and functions of manhood which the younger men now fulfil—Telemachus is an efficient governor, Sir Bedevere's voice will 'Rise like a fountain'—are now forever denied the poems' heroes. Impotent to solve the problem created by the women, and consequently powerless to perform the social tasks required of their sex and position—'this useless hand', Tiresias says—Tennyson's old men can find in death their only destiny, a longed-for dissolution into quietude and inanimation. Each poem articulates this longing for rest in terms of an ideal landscape of either pastoral or chivalric convention in which the speaker is passively absorbed into the scene: 'Take me up . . . And lap me deep within the lonely west' (25–7), is Tithonus's cry, and in the inversions of Arthur's departing words—'I am going a long way . . . Where falls not hail, or rain, or any snow, / Nor ever wind blows loudly' (256–61)—is all the sense of distance, fatigue and failure these poems are centred on.

Tennyson's grief for Hallam, his loss of this most dear friend, precipitated an anxiety expressed in these monologue poems about both masculine competence and manly function. This anxiety was narratively developed and concluded, in a manner characteristic of Tennyson's frequent need at a later stage in his life to rework his early themes within an enlarged social context, in a poem of thirty years later, 'Enoch Arden' (1864), the story of a 'strong heroic soul' whose name, like Adam Bede's, suggests an essence of English manhood. The poem employs familiar Tennysonian motifs: childhood sweethearts, a triangle of lovers, and a test of courage and endurance which is also a suicide bid. Additionally, as Ricks points out, the poem 'brings to a climax' (Ricks 1969; p. 1129) another lifelong preoccupation, the return of the dead to see their place as husband, father and man of property taken by others.

In *Adam Bede*, George Eliot was content to leave her triangle of lovers in harmony, albeit slightly ambivalently so, at the end of the novel. 'Enoch Arden' forces a crisis of competition and completion upon a similar situation. In other poems which treat of rivalrous lovers—*The Lover's Tale*, 'Locksley Hall', *Maud*, *Idylls of the King*, for example— the hero's failure to win and keep the woman he loves is, at least partially, explained by his weakness, particularly by a quality of effeminacy such as Tristram notices in Arthur: 'Man, is he man at all?' ('The Last Tournament',658). But there are no such doubts about Enoch. His manliness is established early in the poem; he is 'stronger-made' and more aggressive than Philip, with weather-beaten face, a bold and successful fisherman. Unlike Philip, who inherits property, Enoch is a self-made man who in his thrift, resourcefulness and domestic reverence exemplifies all the virtues of mid-Victorian capitalist enterprise:

> Enoch set
> A purpose evermore before his eyes,
> To hoard all savings to the uttermost,
> To purchase his own boat, and make a home
> For Annie:
>
> (44–8)

Naturally, Annie loves him in preference to the effeminate and Seth-like Philip.

There are sufficient external causal factors, including that same spirit of enterprise which made him so proper a man, to account for Enoch's disappearance and eventual death. Trading ventures and the misfortunes that could overtake them were issues sympathetically familiar to the Victorian reading public. Yet the perverseness of Enoch's decision to leave his family, the excess and disproportion of his act, is very evident in the poem. Of course, his stubborn determination is seen as an exercise in rightful husbandly authority, but beyond that is the recognition that in the question of Enoch's identity as a man, his wife, children and home operate more forcefully as an emblem, an image carried in the mind's eye to strengthen the resolve of manliness, than as a reality. Indeed, the reality has become mysteriously burdensome and debilitating. Enoch's investment in his family as an image is powerfully suggested in the

description of how he builds and equips Annie's shop before
he leaves her:

> [He bought] Annie goods and stores, and set his hand
> To fit their little streetward sitting-room
> With shelf and corner for the goods and stores.
>   . . . and his careful hand,—
> The space was narrow,—having ordered all
> Almost as neat and close as Nature packs
> Her blossom or her seedling, paused; and he,
> Who needs would work for Annie to the last,
> Ascending tired, heavily slept till morn.
>
> (169–81)

The passage emphasizes the connection between his home
and the trading enterprise he deserts it for; he colonizes and
appropriates the space his absence leaves just as he intends to
colonize and impregnate the vacant places he sets sail for.
The allusion to Nature's economy and her fecundity—'as
neat and close as Nature packs . . . her seedling'—reflects the
containment (his family as image) and potential growth (in
memory) of his action whilst lending the transaction a
softeningly organic yet revealingly sexual colouring. Enoch's
attempts to fill Annie with merchandise as surrogate for his
sexual presence, to replace with goods what his masculinity
can no longer supply, are congruent with the violent urgency
of his departure. It is a destructive urge which has some
similarity to Leontes' need, in *The Winter's Tale*, to break
the ordered pattern of his life and cancel the bonds of
husband and father. As with Leontes, this compulsion
coincides with the birth of another child; significantly in
Enoch's case it is a puny baby boy who will soon die. Annie's
Cassandra-like warning, 'well know I / That I shall look upon
your face no more' (211–12), is heeded as little as any such
woman's cry throughout history by men bent on self-
destruction.

Enoch's exile is to a timeless, ahistorical world of nature,
an 'eternal summer' reminiscent of the island in 'The Lotos-
Eaters' and, like the speakers in that earlier poem, he stands
in relation to his former life as both haunted and haunter:

Dear is the memory of our wedded lives,
And dear the last embraces of our wives
And their warm tears: but all hath suffered change:
        . . . our looks are strange:
And we should come like ghosts to trouble joy.
                    ('The Lotos-Eaters',114–19)

When Enoch does return to the world of manhood responsibilities it is in just such a changed state, as a ghost, effectively
absent yet uncannily present. His absent-presence is powerfully captured in two complementary passages describing,
firstly, his children's estranged vision of him:

              for Enoch seemed to them
Uncertain as a vision or a dream,
Faint as a figure seen in early dawn
Down at the far end of an avenue,
Going we know not where:
                            (352–6)

and his stranger's vision of them:

Now when the dead man come to life beheld
His wife his wife no more, and saw the babe
Hers, yet not his, upon the father's knee . . .
And him, that other, reigning in his place,
Lord of his rights and of his children's love . . .
                            (754–60)

But the most important result of Enoch's exile is the
prohibition upon speech it imposes, particularly the speech
of social intercourse. He can tell Miriam Lane of his solitary
experiences on the island but when Miriam tells him 'all the
story of his house', it is only her final words about himself
that he 'pathetically, / Repeated muttering "cast away and
lost;" / Again in deepest inward whispers "lost!"' (710–12).
Above all, since she represents all that he has forsaken, he
cannot speak to Annie: 'Not to tell her, never to let her know'
(794).

'Enoch Arden' was immensely popular during its own

period but has since been much abused as the worst kind of Laureate writing, popularly pious and embarrassingly sentimental. The extreme reactions it has caused seem to point to an excessive discrepancy between the ostensible meaning of the poem and its subterranean obsessions; for 'Enoch Arden' as a story of noble, heroic manhood is also a fascinating dramatization of an anxiety at the heart of male self-esteem: the anxiety that men, even the best and bravest, could fail in masculinity, and therefore in manliness, and that in ways not readily understood this is a failure to be desired. Not only the wilfulness of Enoch's exile but the weighting of the story towards his home-coming (in this it is a significant development from 'The Lotos-Eaters') suggest that the exile represents something of great desirability as well as of fear, and of such enormity that it 'haunts' the story ever afterwards. Enoch's ghost, like any other guilty and unquiet thing, with increasing intensity haunts the scene of his 'crime': as an absence neither living nor dead during his years on the island, as a living ghost on his return to his home village, and then as a legendary ghost after his death. As such a ghost, he is both familiar and strange; he is, in fact, uncanny. As Freud says, 'the uncanny is in reality nothing new or alien, but something which is familiar and old-established in the mind ... the uncanny [is] something which ought to have remained hidden but has come to light' (Freud 1955a; p. 241). Enoch does indeed 'come to light'; in the proper order of things he ought to have perished at sea with his colleagues but as a ghost he returns to take alien and uncanny possession of his familiar landscape. His apparently benign prohibition on Annie not to visit him ('For my dead face would vex her afterlife' (887)) is in effect an unremovable curse; it oddly recalls Kent's words on the dying Lear—'Vex not his ghost. O! Let him pass' (*King Lear* V.iii.312)—, but in Tennyson's poem it will be the ghost of the young Enoch, not the dead man but the younger one who left her at the prime of his manhood, that will trouble the living woman and will not let her pass beyond that far-off moment of his desertion. His final and terrible revenge upon the family and community he transgressed so many years before is the

'token' of his dead baby's hair by which Annie's new baby is
illegitimized, her marriage to Philip made bigamous and his
children fathered by a corpse:

> But if my children care to see me dead,
> Who hardly knew me living, let them come,
> I am their father;
>
> (884–6)

If, like Tithonus, Ulysses and the other 'strong, heroic' men
of Tennyson's poems, Enoch wills his own death, it follows
that this desired annihilation expresses a revulsion against
life, against living the life of a man with the responsibilities of
'head and ruler' (in Acton's words), and perhaps also a
revulsion within masculinity itself, a dark and annihilative
centre to male sexuality. 'Everything dies for *internal*
reasons', says Freud, and 'the aim of all life is death' (Freud
1955b; p. 38).

Freud's theory of the death instinct seems to be modelled
on a pattern of male sexual activity in which loss and void are
implicated in satisfaction; although such a theory ill fits
female experience, its very androcentricity offers real insights into Enoch's case. At the point when Enoch seems to
have achieved satisfaction in the ways Yeats describes in
'What Then?'—'All his happier dreams come true—/ A small
old house, wife, daughter, son, / Grounds where plum and
cabbage grew'—, the point when the sexual instinct, Eros, is
fulfilled, then the conservative or death instinct, the urge
inherent in organic life 'to restore an earlier state of things'
asserts itself:

> Is it really the case that, *apart from the sexual instincts*, there are
> no instincts that do not seek to restore an earlier state of things
> which has never yet been attained? I know of no certain example
> from the organic world that would contradict the characteriza-
> tion I have thus proposed .... The present development of
> human beings requires, as it seems to me, no different explana-
> tion from that of animals. (Freud 1955b; pp. 41–2)

Enoch's weakling child, the surrogacy of his sexual relations
with Annie, his fall from his boat, the failure of his business

enterprise, imply a slackening of the tension between the life and death instincts, a failure in the masculinity necessary to keep the regressive impulses at bay. The climax of his self-made manhood is reached at the end of 'Seven happy years of health and competence, / And mutual love and honourable toil' (82–3) and what remains beyond this point of optimum drive is the need to escape from social and sexual life into an absorption into landscape, into the inanimate world from which life derives. The only 'desire' Enoch now can have is the desire to die. But this is both so deep an urge and so transgressive a wish that it must be repressed and the only expression it is allowed in the poem is as an interlude, the time on the island, and as a haunting, an uncanny presence, the return of the dead.

The concluding lines of 'Enoch Arden' have always aroused derision:

> So past the strong heroic soul away.
> And when they buried him the little port
> Had seldom seen a costlier funeral.

Tennyson defended them by saying that 'The costly funeral is all that poor Annie could do for him after he was gone. This is entirely introduced for her sake, and, in my opinion, quite necessary to the perfection of the Poem and the simplicity of the narrative' (Ricks 1969; p. 1152). Indeed, the ending is a necessary recognition that this has been a poem about a haunting and an exorcism, a costly burial of the repression of Enoch's 'crime' and an attempt to rid Annie of her curse. 'Enoch Arden' is also Tennyson's own burial of his obsession; it is the last of his poems to be concerned with the return of the dead (Arthur's return is a distant hope not a present fear) and the one that most clearly, schematically almost, brings the crime of self-annihilation and its repression face to face. In the future, the problem of manhood will not go away, indeed it will be of paramount concern in *Idylls of the King*, but the crime of admitting its frailty and destructiveness, of speaking the unspeakable truth of its deathward destiny, has been buried with Enoch.

CHAPTER FOUR

Weak Men and the Discourse of Weakness

Those who are so careful that women should not become men, do not see that men are becoming, what they have decided that women should be—are falling into the feebleness which they have so long cultivated in their companions. Those who are associated in their lives, tend to become assimilated in character. In the present closeness of association between the sexes, men cannot retain manliness unless women acquire it. (Harriet Taylor, 'The Enfranchisement of Women')

> ... this high gift of strength committed to me ...
> Under the Seal of silence could not keep,
> But weakly to a woman must reveal it ...
> (Milton, *Samson Agonistes*)

Most of Tennyson's heroes are not like Enoch Arden. The 'long and listless boy / Late left an orphan of the squire' of 'The Miller's Daughter' (1832) and the 'shining streams of girlish curls' of the lover in 'The Gardener's Daughter' (1842) inaugurate a line of effeminate protagonists who culminate in Arthur, the 'eunuch-hearted king' of *Idylls of the King*. Most notable of these effeminate young men, who with the ambiguous exception of Arthur have not yet accepted the responsibilities and dignity of manhood, are the hero of *The Princess*—'A prince I was, blue-eyed, and fair in face ... With lengths of yellow ringlets like a girl' (I.1–3)—, the passionate, morbid and hysterical hero of *Maud*, and the mourner of *In Memoriam* whose weakness, tears, sighs, faintness, self-doubt and dependency cast him, as he frequently casts himself, in a female role.

In each of these cases, the protagonist arrives by the end of the poem at a state of manliness which has been sought for, through the mediating force of love, throughout the poem. The Prince's final words in *The Princess*—'Accomplish thou my manhood and thyself; / Lay they sweet hands in mine and trust in me'—are replete with manly assurance and authority. In *Maud* the protagonist's pleas 'for a man to arise in me, / That the man I am may cease to be!' (I.396–7) is granted; although he does not finally possess his beloved, the chivalric code she represents inspires him to throw off his 'old hysterical mock-disease' and 'cleave . . . to a cause that I felt to be pure and true' (III.31–3). The course of *In Memoriam* is marked by the mourner's struggle to quell his 'wild and wandering cries', no longer to be 'the fool of loss' but to assume the genial, fatherly assurance of the speaker in the Epilogue, a man who can command a social occasion, make new friends and tame his grief, 'like a statue solid-set, / And moulded in colossal calm' (Epil. 15–16). As this quotation from *In Memoriam* implies, Tennyson subscribes to the notion that the acquisition of manhood imposes restraint of emotion and, as a corollary, of speech. Tennyson's speakers fall silent when their manhood is attained; their poetic utterance ends as they enter the public world of action and authority. The 'silence' of manliness, is, of course, of a particular kind; if a sequel to *The Princess* could be imagined, there is no doubt that in it the Prince would be talking his head off, but it would be the public utterance of a manly life, not the voice of the emotions and, therefore, of poetry.

The shortcomings of manliness in respect of what could be said, and how, are obvious in relation to poetry in Tennyson's understanding of it. Emotional excess, heightened sensibility and expressive language, the stuff of poetry in the Romantic tradition to which Tennyson belonged, are incompatible with manliness in its mid-nineteenth-century definitions. Although such definitions may not pose a problem for the realist novelist, may indeed provide her with her theme, as they did for George Eliot in *Adam Bede*, they are a grave limitation on a lyric poet. The literary legacy Tennyson inherited stressed the specially sensitive and emotional nature of the poet; he is, said Wordsworth in the Preface to *Lyrical Ballads*, 'endued with more lively sensibility, more enthusiasm and tenderness . . . an ability of conjuring up in himself passions . . . a greater readiness and power in expressing what he thinks and feels'. Coleridge, although more cautiously, likewise emphasized the poet's 'more than usual state of emotion . . . and feeling profound and vehement' (*Biographia Literaria*, XIV).

For Tennyson, these ideas were forcefully summarized in 1835 in an important review of his early poetry by J.S. Mill. What the poet possesses, Mill claims, is

> a nervous organization . . . so constituted, as to be, more easily than common organizations, thrown, either by physical or moral causes, into *states* of enjoyment or suffering . . . . This peculiar kind of nervous susceptibility seems to be the distinctive character of the poetic temperament. It constitutes the capacity for poetry; (quoted Jump 1967; p. 91)

During a period when the separate spheres and sexual categories were being rigidly defined, when there prevailed what Weeks calls 'a gospel of real manhood and real womanhood' in which 'women were increasingly associated with weakness and emotion [and] by 1860 men no longer dared embrace in public or shed tears' (Weeks 1981; p. 40), a poet of Tennyson's allegiances found himself confronted not only by the kind of moral questions concerning manliness that George Eliot faced but by a poetic dilemma also. Enjoined by his society to endorse the active and public virtues of manhood—'A life in civic action warm. . . A potent voice of Parliament, / A pillar steadfast in the storm' (*In Memoriam* CXIII.9–12)—, he had nevertheless been exorted by those whose writings he most admired, including Arthur Hallam, to be a poet 'in the highest and truest sense', one who would be susceptible of the slightest impulse . . . trembl[ing] into emotion at colours, and sounds, and movements' (quoted Jump ibid. pp. 36–7).

For the young Tennyson, access to the expression of this heightened sensibility seems to have been most readily gained by his use of female personaê in the several poems he called simply by a woman's name: 'Claribel', 'Isabel', 'Mariana', and so on. This use of female figures had been sanctioned by the poetic theory and practice of his Romantic predecessors whose belief in the chameleon-like nature of the imagination, its 'esemplastic power', encouraged sexual indeterminacy and poetic transvestitism. In poems like 'The Thorn', 'The Mad Mother' and 'The Female Vagrant', Wordsworth had shown how the experiences of poor country-women of the late eighteenth-century could provide a vehicle for the poet's heightened apprehension of solitude and desertion.

Tennyson's early 'lady' poems, 'evolved, like the camel, from my own consciousness' (Ricks 1969; p. 181), adopt the postures of Regency and early Victorian maidenhood and whilst they obviously enable Tennyson voyeuristically to delineate and categorize feminine types, they are also, as his own comment suggests, to do with his consciousness and growth as a poet. Each woman offers the opportunity for a poetic exercise in which Tennyson could both practice his technique and also display attitudes, explore moods and indulge in fancies. They belong particularly to the undergraduate phase of Tennyson's career, the apprentice work of a young poet, interesting and slightly puzzling in that there are so many. They suggest an obsessional concern with women not only as objects to be written about but also as subjective states to be entered into.

Tennyson never lost his obsession with women, but by the time he left Cambridge he had begun to frame and contextualize his 'ladies'. The poems of evocation of female types cease by 1831 and are overtaken by poems of narrative in which increasingly the lady is part of a courtship or marriage story. One of the earliest of the narrative poems is 'The Lady of Shalott' and this establishes a pattern of lovers meeting, usually with disastrous results, in which, as in *Maud* and *Idylls of the King*, the lady more and more performs an iconographic function in a drama of male power and need. In a famous essay of 1948, Lionel Stevenson was the first to notice Tennyson's obsession with women and the evolution of this obsession; in particular Stevenson drew attention to the way in which 'the image of an isolated and unhappy maiden [recurred] with a persistence [which] inevitably suggests a psychological interpretation'. Stevenson employed a Jungian interpretation in which the maiden is seen as the archetypal image of the *anima*, the symbol of the unconscious, always represented in Jungian psychology by the opposite sex. Stevenson read Tennyson's use of this symbol as 'an unintentional diary of his psychological evolution' through three stages from the first stirrings of the *anima*, to identification of it as an unconscious force in conflict with his rational will, to an emotional stability in which the mysterious maiden is objectified and reduced to a 'matter-of-fact literary stock character' (Stevenson 1967; p. 135–6).

Whilst Stevenson is right in noticing the way in which Tennyson increasingly distances himself from his female characters, to assume that this implies an emotional stability is to miss something else that happens in his poetry, which is that the attitudes and neuroses embodied in the female figures in his early work become more consistently located in the young male protagonists of his later poems, who are as weak, emotional, dependent and at times hysterical as any of Tennyson's female characters. Effeminate men are occasionally present in early poems such as 'Supposed Confessions', 'If I Were Loved', and *The Lover's Tale*, but by the time of 'Locksley Hall' (1842) these figures have become a settled feature of Tennyson's verse and the kind of consciousness they possess has become the dominant one. It is interesting that as attitudes hardened towards manhood and womanhood, Tennyson could persist in the deployment of such unmanly figures as the protagonists of *The Princess* and *Maud*. But of course these young men are on their way to becoming manly: they acknowledge their inadequacy—'At war with myself ... Sick, sick to the heart of life, am I' (I.364–5), as the hero of *Maud* says—and strive to overcome it, and so the notion of manhood as a desirable state is not challenged. Although the interest of the story may lie in their inadequacy, manhood as a goal is never explicitly doubted.

The benefit to poetry, however, of the use of an effeminate or feminized protagonist is that it liberates the voice of feeling. As Adam in *Adam Bede* requires Dinah's voice to enable him to express emotion, so Tennyson makes use of a womanly hero, or a womanly voice, to play a similar expressive role within the dynamics of his poetry. This is a procedure most notably developed in *In Memoriam*, the terms of which are governed by the conventions of heterosexual love. This is not to say, except in the very loosest sense, that it is a poem about homosexual love, but rather that in order to talk about close friendship between men, to write an intimate elegy rather than the hyperbolic and distant type of *Lycidas* or *Adonais*, Tennyson could only gain access to the appropriate language of feeling by casting his relationship with Hallam in a heterosexual pattern with himself usually performing the female, wifely role. Since he admired and looked up to Hallam, this role in its Victorian conception was not inappropriate; further, it empowered him to express heightened emotion and to approach the subject of his loss in a way that manliness, with its emphasis on the active virtues and on self-control in speech and behaviour, could not allow.

The question of a relationship between men in which a woman is present as a conduit of the relationship has been explored by Mary Jacobus and, particularly, Eve Kosofsky Sedgwick, who have shown how women are used as 'exchangeable, perhaps symbolic, property for the primary purpose of cementing the bonds of men with men' (Kosofsky Sedgwick 1985; pp. 25–6). This traffic in women operates in the economic, social, sexual—and textual—exchanges men conduct, as, for example, in *The Princess* which can be seen as a poem 'about the enforcement of women's relegation within the framework of male homosocial exchange' (ibid. p. 120). The poem updates the enforcement to replace physical strength and naked dynastic ambition with equally powerful ideological persuasion but this cannot disguise a system in which women are the most valuable counters men can use in their dealings with each other. And as Kosofsky Sedgwick points out, the form of the poem reflects its substance: 'the telling of the story, like a woman, is passed from hand to hand among the young men' (ibid. p. 127). Tennyson's uneasiness at the blatancy of what is happening is articulated in the poem—'I moved as in a strange diagonal, / And maybe neither pleased myself nor them' (Concl.27–8)—and betrayed in the slippages between inner and outer narratives and in the poem's tonal irresolutions.

The conduit procedures in *In Memoriam* are neither so simple nor so obvious. The poem is suffused with female presences, most particularly those which the narrator projects, but these are not the 'exchangeable property' in the way Ida and her woman are; they are not the mere fall guys of a text seeking to bond men together. It is rather the case that female attributes are invaded and appropriated as a means by which male friendship can be celebrated and its demise mourned. The transvestite facility of Tennyson's early years emerges again here to become the vehicle for grief, a conduit of a sort but one which becomes and assimilates, at least temporarily, its proponent. The triangular exchange of men seeking reciprocal adequacy through women, a triangle firmly drawn in *The Princess*, is collapsed in *In Memoriam* by the merging, through metaphor, parallelism, analogue and personification, of the poet-mourner and his female referents. This collapse is a process of unmanning which allows Tennyson to adopt the posture and speech of grief and desire, which in their manly forms are 'unspeakable'. Located either in parallel female figures who present a socially acceptable form of weakness or in an autobiographical effeminacy eventually to be redeemed, his emotion can be not only displayed but also controlled and disciplined. These female selves, who mourn and yearn, and speak their need, can be cajoled, bullied and dismissed, and finally, when sufficient authority over them has been gained, they can be figuratively speaking exchanged, and the bond between men created.

The sexual politics of the poem are initiated by the feminization of the poet's response to Hallam's death. His shocked and weakened state is frequently likened to that of female grievers: the mother and sweetheart of section VI, the female linnet of section XXI, Mary grieving for Lazarus in section XXXI. The resignation of his later bereft state is compared to that of an abandoned or unrequited woman: the 'poor girl' of section LX or the wife of XCVII. These analogues relate to the many sections in which the poet's friendship with the dead man is likened to a married or widowed state; the 'weeds' of IX, the 'widowed hour' of XL and the widowed heart (113) of LXXXV all confirm the conjugacy through which the poet's relationship with his friend is channelled:

> Two partners of a married life—
>   I looked on these and thought of thee
>   In vastness and in mystery,
> And of my spirit as of a wife.
>   (XCVII.5–8)

One rarely, as in sections VIII, XIII and XL, is the relationship reversed, with the dead Hallam likened to a female role, and these occasions are lost in a general impression of the poet as the weaker partner. Tears, prostration, dependency, guilt, faintings, anxiety, a sense of inadequacy and inferiority, these are the features of the poet's self-presentation, particularly in the earlier part of the poem where the narrator's womanly guise is assumed the more readily in order that he may indulge in the throes of grief and the extremes of sensibility.

But this effeminate or womanly self is accompanied by another self whose survival and triumph is a condition of the poem's conclusion. Although obviously gaining strength as his authority over the poem grows and his authorship unfolds and is consolidated, this other 'I', the manly one of Tennyson's two voices, is present throughout the poem to conduct a dialogue with his female counterpart and increasingly to correct and control 'her' excesses. In section XVIII, for example, the sexual play between the two voices begins with a quietly dignified and manly passage, replete with echoes from English and Classical literature, reminders of tradition and received wisdom: ' 'Tis well; 'tis something; we may stand / Where he in English earth is laid . . . And come, whatever loves to weep, / And hear the ritual of the dead' (1–12). But this gives way in stanza four to the expressive feminized 'I' who shatters the ritualized calm of the burial:

> Ah yet, even yet, if this might be,
>   I, falling on his faithful heart,
>   Would breathing through his lips impart
> The life that almost dies in me;

Christopher Ricks suggests that this stanza recalls Elisha's resuscitation of the child in 2 Kings iv.34 (Ricks 1969; p. 881); more powerfully evoked, however, is the faithful wife who flings herself on her dead husband's body. But this image of suttee, so disturbing in its connotations of passion, breakdown and cessation, cannot be allowed full rein. With a characteristic use of enjambment and repetition—'. . . that almost dies in me; / That dies not . . .' (16–17)—the section is rescued from collapse and the narrator's self-control is recovered: 'And slowly forms the firmer mind' (18).

A different form of the dialogue between the feminized poetic self and a male control occurs in section LXXVII:

> What hope is there for modern rhyme
>   To him, who turns a musing eye
>   On songs, and deeds, and lives, that lie
> Foreshortened in the tract of time?
>
> These mortal lullabies of pain
>   May bind a book, may line a box,
>   May serve to curl a maiden's locks;
> Or when a thousand moons shall wane
>
> A man upon a stall may find,
>   And, passing, turn the page that tells
>   A grief, then changed to something else,
> Sung by a long-forgotten mind.
>
> But what of that? My darkened ways
>   Shall ring with music all the same;

>   To breathe my loss is more than fame,
>   To utter love more sweet than praise.

Here the debate is seen in terms of history, represented by the indifferent, browsing man who turns its pages, and what is left out of history, the breath and utterance of 'long-forgotten mind[s]', the probable fate of the poet's songs. In his self-effacement, the poet's conception of his worth is inevitably feminized; his songs are lullabies, and their future is domestic and marginalized: 'May bind a book, may line a box, / May serve to curl a maiden's locks'. In this section, one of the most poignant of *In Memoriam*, the expressive but private and unauthorized world of female utterance is permitted a temporary superiority over the values of a public life: 'To breathe my loss is more than fame, / To utter loss more sweet than praise.'

Until towards the end of *In Memoriam*, the control the 'firmer mind' is able to exert over the wayward emotions of its feminized counterpart is precarious and constantly threatened, as the midway and probably most despairing group of sections, L–LVI, demonstrates. The argument of this group is a circular one, starting from the plea to Hallam to 'Be near me', and concluding with a similar desire for 'thy voice to soothe and bless'. Contained within this personalized expression of fear and inadequacy, and of the need for Hallam's physical presence to reassure the narrator, are statements about the general pain and evil in the world, about Nature's indifference to these, and of their bearing on human existence. In this swift and solipsistic movement from the personal to the cosmic, which is also an attempt to rationalize and objectify the panic registered by the narrator's weaker self, Tennyson employs the two voices of his sexualized dialogue with disconcerting results. The feminized dependency and self-abasement of Sections L and LI are mildly reproved and dismissed as the 'plaintive song' and self-absorption of someone who is weak and immature, as the frettings of an 'idle girl' (LII.13). But this implicit admonition to 'be a man' entails the recognition that 'life is dashed with flecks of sin' which, in a highly Victorian association, means sexual sin, particularly the 'wild oat' of the double standard:

> How many a father have I seen,
>   A sober man, among his boys,
>   Whose youth was full of foolish noise,
> Who wears his manhood hale and green;
>
> And dare we to this fancy give,
>   That had the wild oat not been sown,
>   The soil, left barren, scarce had grown
> The grain by which a man may live?
>   (LIII.1–8)

But this apparently reassuring father-figure, once slightly wayward but now a respectable sire, seems to precipitate an anxiety which reduces the narrator to 'An infant crying in the night' (LIV.18), a faltering supplicant on 'the great world's altar-stairs', a despairing mystic whose only 'hope of answer or redress' lies 'Behind the veil, behind the veil' (LVI.26–7).

The inference to be drawn from this group is that the putting aside of effeminacy necessary to the acquisition of manhood also reduces the possibility of attaining to a certain kind of goodness, namely, the virtue exemplified in Christ's way of life: 'the sinless years / That breathed beneath the Syrian blue' (LII.11–12). It is the Adam-Seth dichotomy again; sexual purity and sensitivity of feeling preclude manliness, and vice versa. A man's burden of masculinity, Adam's burden, carries with it an infection, 'pangs of nature, sins of will, / Defects of doubt, and taints of blood (LIV.3–4), and it is the anxiety caused by this knowledge that the narrator's collapse into infancy or mysticism registers. The presence in this group of the threatening female presences of Philosophy and Nature demonstrates the extremity of Tennyson's unease; conspirators in the narrator's dilemma as procuress, wanton or demon, they are both symptom and cause of the problem, figures in a violent nightmare of sexual difference. The ontological questions this group of sections apparently addresses seem, after all, to dissolve into questions of sexual identity and control.

The late group CIX–CXIV provides a development of the male-female dialogue which appears to achieve a reconciliation of its oppositions. The concern of the group is to praise Hallam, both as he was and as he might have been, and to cast him in the role of ideal man, a true 'gentleman'. He emerges as a brilliant talker and thinker, a liberal moralist, a man of social presence, a leader of others; but along with these obviously manly qualities are those of 'graceful tact' and 'sweetness', 'And manhood fused with female grace' (CIX.17). In Hallam this union of tenderness and strength fulfils a prophecy made in *The Princess*:

> Yet in the long years liker must they grow;
> The man be more of woman, she of man;
> He gain in sweetness and in moral height,
> Nor lose the wrestling thews that throw the world;
>   (VII.263–6)

In the coming age of human progress, which Hallam's excellence foreshadows, men will have assimilated the best qualities of women to become better human beings, an apparently ideal programme. But where does this leave women? If they too fuse with men, then an androgynous, egalitarian utopia is at hand. This is not, however, what Tennyson had in mind: 'I prize that soul where man and woman meet ... But, friend, man-woman is not woman-man', he wrote in a late poem, ('On One Who Affected an Effeminate Manner,' 1889), and even in *The Princess*, the most progressive and optimistic of his long poems, the separateness of the sexes is firmly upheld: 'Woman is not undevelopt man, / But diverse ... Not like to like, but like in difference' (VII.259–62). When 'feminist' thinkers like Hallam advocated the cause of women by claiming their good influence on men—'women's love was sent to chasten us for heaven'—they implicitly raised the question of woman's fate once the chastening has taken place, once not just the individual man but the whole race of men have gained 'in sweetness and in moral height'. Hallam did not live long enough to develop the logic of his position, but Tennyson

did explore its implications. The questions Tennyson turns
to in his later poetry, and glances at even in *In Memoriam*,
concern the feminized man, that is the man who unites
manliness with female grace, and the woman whose function
as redeemer of man has been made redundant. The fate of
the Tennysonian woman will be discussed more fully in
Section Three, but it is worth noting that this group of
poems in *In Memoriam* broaches her future in a manner
which anticipates Tennyson's later division of her into
ineffectual angel or dangerous sexual energy, into Elaine or
Guinevere. Sections CX and CXIV suggest the dichotomy.
In CX, as a final projection of the poet's feminized self, the
figure appears of the good wife whose only function is to
admire:

> While I, thy nearest, sat apart,
>   And felt thy triumph was as mine; ...
> Nor mine the sweetness or the skill,
>   But mine the love that will not tire ...
>   (13–18)

But in dangerous proximity to this patriarchal image of ideal
womanhood is the personification of knowledge as female in
section CXIV: 'some wild Pallas from the brain / Of Demons
... fiery-hot to burst / All barriers in her onward race / For
power' (12–15). Tennyson's persistent anxiety towards
knowledge as an uncontrollable force is indicated in his use as
the first stanza of CXIV of four lines (133–6) from one of his
most politically conservative poems of the 1830s, 'Hail
Briton!': 'Who loves not knowledge? who shall rail / Against
her beauty? ... let her work prevail.' In both poems a
distinction is made between knowledge, which is wayward
and earthly, and wisdom, 'the higher hand', 'heavenly of the
soul'. In both Platonic and Biblical tradition wisdom is
invariably female but Tennyson obscures this traditional
usage or, if anything, makes wisdom male by association
with Hallam who 'year and hour [grows] / In reverence
and in charity'. In the scheme of sexual difference in
which Tennyson's moral and political philosophy operates,

knowledge, by which he means an impulsive and uncon-
sidered curiosity, inevitably is female, not only a 'wild Pallas'
but Eve-Pandora also, who in 'Submitting all things to
desire' is a cause of anarchy unless controlled by rationality to
become a moral influence. The image of 'some wild Pallas'
recalls lines in section XXXIV concerning the 'Fantastic
beauty; such as lurks / In some wild Poet, when he works /
Without a conscience or an aim'. In *In Memoriam*, as in *The
Princess*, woman and poet are aligned; the 'true' poet, who
'constantly [feels] sentiments of exquisite pleasure or pain,
which most men [are] not permitted to experience' (Hallam,
quoted Jump 1967; p. 38), and the woman are those forces of
emotion, creativity and unconscious energy which lie outside
of but which feed rationative discourse and which underlie
'conscience' and 'aim'.

In the general movement of the poem, however, the
control of these female forces of emotional excess is essential
to the formation of a proper bond of friendship between
men, between the narrator and his dead friend and the
narrator and other men. Just as Ida's dwindling into
wifehood in *The Princess* is required for the accomplishment
of the Prince's manhood, so the relegation of the female self
in *In Memoriam* to the role of passive admirer or exchangeable property is the necessary condition for the emergence of
a figure of self-possession and manliness who completes the
poem: as the poem says, 'men may rise on stepping-stones /
Of their dead selves to higher things' (I.3). This rise into new
manhood is accelerated in the last fifth of the poem as a
corollary to Hallam's elevation into the figure of an ideal
man, a model to whom both the narrator and succeeding
generations can look for inspiration. This growth is manifest
both in the narrator's acceptance of social responsibilities—'I
will not shut me from my kind ... Nor feed with sighs a
passing wind' (CVIII.1–4)—and in his ability to forge anew
his bond, albeit now a metaphysical and spiritual one,
with his friend, and to consummate this renewed relationship. Their ecstatic union, particularly evident in sections
CXXII, CXXIX and CXXX, has been achieved through the
mediating function of the other self which is still present in

the 'inconsiderate boy' of CXXII.14 and the expressive
endearments of CXXIX—'Sweet human hand and lips and
eye . . . Mine, mine, for ever, ever mine' (6,8)—but which is
now under the control of a dominant, even aggressive,
narrative 'I':

> I have thee still, and I rejoice;
> I prosper, circled with thy voice;
> I shall not lose thee though I die.
> (CXXX.14–16)

The obsolescence of the conduit role of the feminized
personae is recognized in the Epilogue in a final 'exchange'
transaction which completes the poem. This final section, an
Epithalamium, celebrates a new friendship with a man
through the marriage of a sister, a re-enactment of the
exchange which should have more closely bonded the poet
with his dead friend. That prospective marriage is recalled:

> Nor have I felt so much of bliss
>   Since first he told me that he loved
>   A daughter of our house;
>   (5–7)

and a new friendship, already mooted in CXVI.16 ('. . .
some strong bond which is to be'), celebrated. The Epilogue
marks the poet's survival of his loss and his accession to the
world of manly responsibilities; his stance is detached,
fatherly, proprietorial:

> For I that danced her on my knee,
>   That watched her on her nurse's arm,
>   That shielded all her life from harm
> At last must part with her to thee;
>   (45–8)

In this most patriarchal of all acts—the giving away of a
woman by one man to another—the narrator has exchanged
his womanly self which he had earlier identified with a
bereaved sister—'we do him wrong / To sing so wildly: let us

go ...' (LVII.3–4)—for a manly self of action and of emotional and verbal restraint. In this hard-won position of authority it is his prerogative to slough off the weaker, unmanly selves and the truths concerning emotional excess that they had told him:

> For I myself ... have grown
> To something greater than before;
>
> Which makes appear the songs I made
>   As echoes out of weaker times,
>   As half but idle brawling rhymes,
> The sport of random sun and shade.
>   (Epil. 19–24)

Of course, this has to be the conclusion; the poem's substance is the 'idle brawling rhymes', and in the 'sport' with its feminized selves lies its major dynamics.

CHAPTER FIVE

Perfect Men

All I wish for now, said Arthur,
Is the beautiful colour blue
And to ride in the blue sunshine
And Guinevere I do not wish for you. . . .

Yes, Arthur has passed away
Gladly he has laid down his reigning powers
He has gone to ride in the blue light
Of the peculiar towering cornflowers.
    (Stevie Smith, 'The Blue from Heaven')

Perfection is terrible, it cannot have children.
    (Sylvia Plath, 'The Munich Mannequins')

In the figure of Arthur Hallam *In Memoriam* Tennyson
proposed a new man who would comprise the better qualities
of both sexes, a 'manhood fused with female grace', a type he
saw foreshadowed in 'the "man–woman" in Christ, the union
of tenderness and strength' (Tennyson 1897; I.326). This
concept is explored in the figure of King Arthur in *Idylls of
the King*. Similar in appearance to the effeminate heroes of
Tennyson's earlier poems, Arthur is 'fair / Beyond the race of
Britons and of men' ('The Coming of Arthur', 329–30) with
a golden beard ('Merlin and Vivien', 58) and a 'clear face'
like an angel's, and like some of his predecessors, he has
been a kindly childhood companion, as his sister Bellicent
affirms:

> ... he was at my side,
> And spake sweet words, and comforted my heart,
> And dried my tears, being a child with me.
> ... those first days had golden hours for me ...
> ('The Coming of Arthur', 347–56)

Such a tender portrait is a marked development from Tennyson's source in Malory where Arthur's childhood character is ignored and Bellicent's existence, let alone her testimony, is excluded.

The transformation of Malory's medieval king who springs fully-armed upon the narrative by removing the sword from the stone into a loving boy who will grow into the man-woman of Tennyson's conception has been remarked upon by commentators from Swinburne onwards. The deliberation and consistency with which Tennyson held to this conception is indicated by the dedication to the poem, addressed 'To the Prince Consort' and published in 1862, that is, after the publication of the first four *Idylls* ('Vivien', 'Enid', 'Guinevere' and 'Elaine') in 1859 but before the remaining seven books, the bulk of the poem, were written. Albert is seen as a model for the nation's manhood, the 'ideal knight' who images Arthur's own excellence. In character this new man is

> ... modest, kindly, all-accomplished, wise,
> With what sublime repression of himself,
> And in what limits, and how tenderly;
> ... through all this tract of years
> Wearing the white flower of a blameless life ...
> (Dedication, 17–24)

The bourgeoisification of the monarchy, which reached its height during Victoria's reign, held as its central tenet the faithful, affectionate marriage of the Queen and Consort in which domestic virtue and familial responsibility set the pattern for Victorian respectability and marriage idealism. Tennyson has no doubt that in this royal marriage Albert was all that a good husband should be, that is, the primary partner, the support and guide of his wife, in effect, the

King, 'Albert the Good': 'Thou noble Father of [England's]
Kings to be' (33). Victoria's bereft state after Albert's death
is therefore viewed as one of passive endurance; she waits to
resume her role, not of Queen but of wife: 'Till God's love set
Thee at his side again' (53).

The nature of Albert's goodness and of Arthur's imposes
upon them the responsibilities of justice, protection of the
weak and sexual purity: 'Wearing the white flower of a
blameless life' is Albert's description, and Arthur is a 'selfless
man and stainless gentleman' ('Merlin and Vivien', 790).
Faithfulness in marriage is a prerequisite—'Who loved one
only and who clave to her' (Dedication, 10)—, and in Arthur
this becomes a lifelong purity: 'For I was ever virgin save for
thee' ('Guinevere', 554). Although in section LIII of *In
Memoriam* Tennyson could toy with the notion that 'wild
oats' sown in youth ensure a hale and sober manhood, here,
in the ideal figure of Arthur, he is challenging the double
standard, an indication of an increasingly heightened and, in
a newly-emerging sense of the word, feminized concept of
manliness.

Contained in Tennyson's descriptions of both Albert and
Arthur is a development of the notions of manliness
discussed at the beginning of this section: that is, a control
and redirection of masculinity, of the sexual energy which
informs a man's social presence but never dominates it: the
greater the control the greater the fitness to rule, although, as
we saw in *Adam Bede*, this may be at the cost of an ability to
sympathize and communicate. The repression involved in
this concept of manliness is viewed with unstinted
admiration in the Dedication—'With what sublime
repression of himself'—but is more equivocally and
complexly presented in *Idylls of the King* where the 'selfless',
'stainless' character of Arthur, barely requiring self-
repression, carries the notion to a problematic extremity.

Although Tennyson assures us of Arthur's physical
prowess both as a commander of an army, when 'in twelve
great battles [he] overcame / The heathen hordes, and made
a realm and reigned' ('The Coming of Arthur', 517–18), and
in single combat, when he secretly overthrows Balin and

Balan, such instances are rare in *Idylls of the King* and the
weight of Arthur's personal authority rests in his sweetness,
gentleness and purity. Such passive virtues, apparently born
of self-control and forbearance, are now the mark of a good
man; as Arthur himelf says of Edryn's mastery of a violent
temperament and the will and ability to 'pick the vicious
quitch / Of blood and custom wholly out', it is

> A thousand-fold more great and wonderful
> Than if some knight . . .
> Should make an onslaught single on a realm
> Of robbers, though he slew them one by one . . .
> ('Geraint and Enid', 912–17)

The problem is, of course, that we do not see Arthur's
struggle to rid himself of 'the vicious quitch / of blood and
custom'. His feminized, Seth-like asexuality—'Arthur the
blameless, pure as any maid'—entails not only the moral
purity Victorian women supposedly possessed but also their
sexual anaesthesia, their safely denatured generative powers.
For although we should to some extent distrust Guinevere's
opinion that Arthur is 'A moral child without the craft to
rule' ('Lancelot and Elaine', 145), and even more distrust
Garlon's comment that 'ye men of Arthur be but babes'
('Balin and Balan', 356), it is the case that Arthur seems out
of reach of temptation; when Vivien tries to seduce him, he
'gazed upon her blankly' and 'it made the laughter of an
afternoon / That Vivien should attempt the blameless King'
('Merlin and Vivien', 159–62). The unmanning of Arthur to
render him more kindly and more chaste robs him not only of
virility but also of moral complexity. The infantilization of
women in the Victorian period, to keep them in the revered
subjection of sexual ignorance and purity, seems here to have
infected this conception of an ideal man.

This feminization of Arthur makes of him both a spiritual
and an ineffectual figure, a process Tennyson introduces in
connection with his birth. In Malory, although Arthur is
conceived illegitimately and reared by other than his parents,
there is no doubt he is King Uther's son and his proof of

kingship is clearly and quickly established by his ability
to pull the sword from the stone, an incident Tennyson
omits. Tennyson both obscures and makes more respectable
(and also more violent) Arthur's birth and his claim to the
throne; he may be the legitimate son of Uther, conceived
in an enforced marriage, or the legitimate son of Gorlois
or of Anton or yet again—all is hearsay—he may have been
cast by a wave at Merlin's feet, 'Who stoopt and caught the
babe, and cried "The King! / Here is an heir for Uther"'
('The Coming of Arthur', 384–5). As Elliot L. Gilbert has
pointed out, 'the advent of a king who proposes to reign
without the authorization of patrilineal descent is an extraordinary . . . phenomenon' (Gilbert 1983; p. 867) and so too
is one who appears to derive his power and his history from
mysterious female sources. For whereas Malory's Arthur
obtains his sword during an engagingly human episode with
his foster-brother and the men of his society, Tennyson's
Arthur, according to Bellicent, is given his by the 'mystic,
wonderful' Lady of the Lake who seems to have usurped
divine power:

> a mist
> Of incense curled about her, and her face
> Wellnigh was hidden in the minster gloom;
> . . . she dwells
> Down in a deep; calm, whatsoever storms
> May shake the world, and when the surface rolls,
> Hath power to walk the waters like our Lord.
> ('The Coming of Arthur', 286–93)

In the context of Tennyson's poem, the power of this 'female
king', as Gilbert rightly calls Arthur, is circumscribed and
indirect. Like a good woman, Arthur is of great imaginative
and iconographic importance but in practical terms he is
ineffectual, imprisoned in the female 'goodness' he has
appropriated. The best qualities of womanhood, in its
Victorian definitions, of moral innocence, sexual naïvety and
a Ruskinian withdrawal from the corruption of the world,
inevitably deny political and legislative power to the man
who incorporates them. As Acton had pointed out, virility is

not only 'necessary to give a man that consciousness of his
dignity as head and ruler, and of his importance', but this
dignity and importance 'is absolutely essential to the well-
being of the family, and through it, of Society itself' (quoted
in Weeks 1981; p. 39). Like Seth's, Arthur's goodness ill
fits him to be a head of a family, and 'through it, of Society
itself'. He is like the Christ of William Holman Hunt's
painting, 'The Light of the World' (1851–6), a fraily
beautiful inspirational image, the 'passionate perfection' of
Guinevere's guilty scorn. But the oxymoron of her description summarizes the conflicting aspirations in Tennyson's
conception of an ideal man. In the fallen world of Victorian
sexuality, he who aspires to perfection, or even exceptional
goodness, must be without passion.

Unlike his vigorous counterpart in Malory's *Le Morte
Darthur* Tennyson's Arthur is inactive during much of the
poem and this creates a narrative problem. If the central
figure of a poem is merely a distant ideal, then the action and
the debate must be conducted by subsidiary figures, as
happens around Gloriana in Spenser's *The Faerie Queene*.
In the case of *Idylls of the King*, Arthur is similarly
inspirational but not similarly remote; he is an ideal, but,
Tennyson implies, a realizable ideal: 'the highest and most
human too'. The aim of Spenser's knights in *The Faerie
Queene* is to serve Gloriana; Arthur's knights strive to serve
him too, but they also strive to emulate him, to use him as the
exemplar for their own lives: 'to learn what Arthur meant by
courtesy, / Manhood, and knighthood' ('Balin and Balan',
155–6). This means that although Tennyson can solve the
narrative problem of a passive hero by devolving the action
onto the knights, the ideas on which that action is based—to
do the King's will and *to be more like him*—are incompatible.
If the knights are manfully active, as Arthur's injunctions
and the nature of the narrative require them to be, then by
the very possession of the masculinity which nourishes
manly action, they must be less good and their overall quest
must fail because they cannot be like Arthur. The pattern of
a female king imposes an uneasy residue of masculinity on
the knights; just as one may ask what role is left for women if

men take on their best qualities, so one may ask what is to
become of masculine energy if the best of men denies it. The
explanation for the fall of Camelot the poem most obviously
offers is that it is Guinevere's fault; but equally the knights
are responsible for the fall of Camelot. They are misled and
deceived by females like Ettare and Vivien but their vulnerability to such wiles lies in a masculinity that is rendered
problematic by Arthur's asexual perfection. Of all the
knights, the boy Gareth is the only one who wears his
maleness easily yet even his coming of age is given a coyness
which suggests Tennyson's unease at committing this true
nephew of Arthur, whose wish it is to 'Live pure, speak true,
right wrong, follow the King' ('Gareth and Lynette', 117), to
sexual experience;

> And he that told the tale in older times
> Says that Sir Gareth wedded Lyonors,
> But he, that told it later, says Lynette.
> (1392–4)

The other knights range through a variety of troubled
manhood from the risky hedonism of Tristram, who is
slaughtered for his sexual prowess, to the tortured passion of
Lancelot, so pale and depleted a figure in *Idylls of the King* in
comparison with the figures of that name in medieval
romance. How hazardous a world of guilty sexuality Arthur
bestows upon his knights is best illustrated in one of the most
schematic and symbolic of the books of *Idylls of the King*,
'Balin and Balan'.

The landscape of this *Idyll* is highly sexually suggestive,
with shadowy, sliding spears, blood-tipped lances, the dead
bones of relics in King Pellam's all-male court, bowers of
lilies and roses, and a fountain spring 'that down, / From
underneath a plume of lady-fern, / Sang', on either side of
which Arthur finds the twins Balin and Balan who, having
'lain together in one womb', are destined to die together. In
Malory's poem, the punning proximity of 'tomb' and 'womb'
is humourously exploited: 'We came both out of one tomb,
that is to say one mother's belly, and so shall we lie both in

one pit.' But Tennyson avoids this obvious play of words and in the closing lines of the poem establishes instead an oblique and shadowy connection between tomb and womb through his repeated use of the word 'doom':

> 'O brother' answered Balin 'woe is me!
> My madness all thy life has been thy doom,
> Thy curse, and darkened all thy day; and now
> The night has come. I scarce can see thee now.
> Goodnight! for we shall never bid again
> Goodmorrow—Dark my doom was here, and dark
> It will be there. I see thee now no more.
> I would not mine again should darken thine,
> Goodnight, true brother.'
>   Balan answered low
> 'Goodnight, true brother here! goodmorrow there!
> We two were born together, and we die
> Together by one doom;' and while he spoke
> Closed his death-drowsing eyes, and slept the sleep
> With Balin, either locked in either's arm.
>   (607–20)

Unlike Malory's version, in which Balan enters the story late and randomly kills Balin, Tennyson's story links the brothers from the beginning as inseparable, Self and Other, but a Self and Other locked in the inescapable disjunction of the 'wrong' letter of their names: Balin and Balan. This story of a doomed twin relationship is Tennyson's last attempt (published in 1885, although written in 1872) to write out of himself an obsession which, as we have seen, was with him from the early days of *The Lover's Tale*. In some of the other poems on this theme—*Maud* and 'Aylmer's Field', for example—external factors are at least partially the cause of the destruction of the childhood bond, but in this poem, although some blame is attached to Guinevere and Vivien, there is the acknowledgement of the primary cause as being within the self, or *between* the Self and its Other which cannot recognize each other, which can neither acknowledge nor forget their separateness: 'O Balin, Balin,' cries Balan, 'I that fain had died / To save thy life, have brought thee to thy

death. / Why had ye not the shield I knew?' (588–90).
Although each of the brothers' faces is 'Familiar up from
cradle-time', such familiarity can only truly belong to the
narcissism of infancy and is now lost, obscured and disguised,
quite literally, by the masks of adult knighthood Balin and
Balan must wear. To destroy those masks, to pierce the
armour, becomes an attempt to recover that lost wholeness of
infancy which, if successful, is to be born again but into a
birth which will forego development beyond itself, which
will become death. Tennyson movingly invokes the moment
at which wholeness, the doubleness of the twinned soul, and
its impending loss, are registered:

> Balin first woke, and seeing that true face,
> Familiar up from cradle-time, so wan,
> Crawled slowly with low moans to where he lay,
> And on his dying brother cast himself
> Dying; and *he* lifted faint eyes; he felt
> One near him; all at once they found the world,
> Staring wild-wide; then with a childlike wail,
> And drawing down the dim disastrous brow
> That o'er him hung, he kissed it, moaned and spake;
> (579–87)

For Balin, the intolerable loneliness of the 'i' of his name is
resolved in death when he is no longer conscious of
separation from Balan: 'I see thee now no more', he says, on
the point of dying. Balan's facile response, 'Goodnight, true
brother here! goodmorrow there!', attempts to impose a
Christian conclusion on Balin's perception that completion is
also extinction. But the poem cannot bring itself to endorse
either Balin's or Balan's expectation but despairingly reiter-
ates its own truth, that whatever the brothers' future, they
are imprisoned forever in their disjunctive bond, 'either
locked in either's arm'.

This *Idyll*, however, does offer an explanation for the
apparently hopeless situation whereby, on a simple level,
brothers cannot help killing each other, and in a psychoanalytic interpretation, the male self cannot live in harmony
within itself. Tennyson's drift in this respect can be glimpsed

in the revisions he made to the exploits of Malory's Balin who
although causing much destruction is seen as admirable, not
least by Arthur who admits he has wrongly imprisoned him:
'Balin passeth of prowess of any knight, that ever I found,
for much beholden I am unto him.' Tennyson's Arthur
interprets this 'prowess' as 'thy too fierce manhood', has
named Balin 'the Savage', and has justly imprisoned him for
wounding a servant. In Tennyson's interpretation it is not
bad luck or magic swords which impel Balin to disaster (as it
is in Malory) but a turbulent and unmoderated masculinity.
'My father hath begotten me in his wrath' (278), Balin says,
and this pure maleness, which seems apparently to have had
no mothering in the making of it, cannot moderate itself into
social manliness, cannot learn from Lancelot, for instance,
how to 'Make a knight or churl or child or damsel seem /
From being smiled at happier'(159–60). Though he seeks
the female in Guinevere's favour and in Vivien's advice, and,
most significantly, with Balan, 'statuelike', guarding the
'spring . . . underneath a plume of lady-fern', he receives no
redemption, being fooled or baffled by the women and
defeated by Arthur at the spring. In the feminized court of
Camelot he can find neither true womanhood—Guinevere
disillusions him by her dalliance with Lancelot—nor the
manhood he hoped for in Arthur: 'the King / So prizes—
overprizes—gentleness' (179–80). Motherless and father-
less, he finds no model in Camelot for the coexistence of Self
and Other; when Balan leaves him, he becomes a violent
half-self, in whom self-control is a mockery: 'Shall I not
rather prove . . . Fierier and stormier from restraining, break
/ Into some madness . . . ?' (223–5). In the psychosexual
scheme of the poem, it is inevitable that Balan will mistake
Balin, his other self of unmitigated masculinity, for the
'demon of the woods' who 'lived alone, and came / To learn
black magic, and to hate his kind / With such a hate' (123–5).
   As a poem, 'Balin and Balan' seems to arrive at a painful if
honest deduction: Arthur's shining perfection, so idealistically sought for through Tennyson's earlier work, paradoxically casts shadows which incriminate all other members
of the court; his asexual self serves to sharpen sexual

differences, and, as the doomed Balin and Balan relationship shows, renders the possibility of a blurring and softening of the sexual polarities more remote than before. In Arthur's society, the men are barren misogynists like Pellam, cynical villains like Garlon, tortured deceivers like Lancelot or foolish boys like Vivien's squire, Sir Chick. What hope for Balin, seeking an undivided male self, seeking to translate his masculinity into manliness?

SECTION C: WOMEN

CHAPTER SIX

Mariana and the Nature of Woman

Alfred is dreadfully embarrassed with women alone—for he entertains at one and the same moment a feeling of almost adoration for them and an ineffable contempt! adoration for what they *might be*—contempt for what they *are*! (Jane Welsh Carlyle, *Letters to her Family, 1839–1863*)

... be thou as chaste as ice, as pure as snow, thou shalt not escape calumny; get thee to a nunnery ... Or if thou wilt needs marry, marry a fool, for wise men know well enough what monsters you make of them: (*Hamlet*, III.i.138–42)

No English poet has written more about women than Tennyson. As a young poet practising his craft, he seems to have turned to portraits of women as another poet might have written of landscape. His youthful gallery of ladies— 'Claribel', 'Lilian', 'Madeline', 'Amy', and so on—are both technical exercises of some virtuosity and images of a range of early nineteenth-century female types. They are images, rather than simple descriptions, because of Tennyson's ability to isolate and embellish a stance, a gesture, an outline, so that the form of the woman becomes a perfect and memorable representation of the idea of her:

> She, looking through and through me ...
>   Smiling, never speaks:
> So innocent-arch, so cunning-simple,

101

From beneath her gathered wimple
Glancing with black-beaded eyes . . .
('Lilian', 10–15)

Amongst coquettes like Lilian, saints like Isabel and Amy,
and spirited and haughty girls like Rosalind and Kate, in
Tennyson's early poetry there emerges a group of women
who are frustratedly trapped in a situation which has to do
with being female, sometimes mysteriously so: 'Mariana',
'Mariana in the South', 'Œnone', 'Fatima', 'A Dream of Fair
Women' and, of course, 'The Lady of Shalott', who, as Nina
Auerbach has suggested, summarizes the type for all time:
'We may allegorize her into the artist, the poet's anima, a
fragile divinity, an heretical anti-divinity . . . but she carries a
suggestive resonance beyond these classifications, weaving a
myth that belongs to her alone . . . [a] mysterious amalgam of
imprisonment and power' (Auerbach 1982; p. 11). She casts
a long shadow into Tennyson's future poetry as the woman
who waits to be released by a man from a sterile self-
absorption and inactivity into marriage or into death. The
heroines of 'The Miller's Daughter', 'The Gardener's
Daughter', 'The Sleeping Beauty' and *The Princess* are set
free by marriage. Death is the alternative release, either
achieved or desired, for those like Fatima, Œnone, Maud
and Elaine, whom the lover fails. In either case it is the
waiting for deliverance, the suspenseful moment before
fulfilment, which yields both romantic and erotic
enthralment: 'She is coming, my life, my fate . . . she is near,
she is near' (*Maud* I.911–12), and it is the 'coming' of the
woman that Tennyson's poetry celebrates. Yet the essence of
such coming is that it has to be transformed into an image;
fixed and possessed by the poet's technique, its sexual
display is available for leisurely surveillance by the reader.
And as John Berger has pointed out in his survey of the
European nude in painting, 'the spectator in front of the
picture . . . is assumed to be a man'; nudes in painting, like
Tennyson's women, are 'offering up [their] femininity as the
surveyed' (Berger 1972; pp. 54–5).
    In 'The Gardener's Daughter' (1842; composed 1833–4)

the girl is displayed with loosened hair and arm aloft, and the
reader's specular caress is invited through the male touching
of her body by the day, and by the poet's acknowledgement
that his words make of her an image—'such a breast / As
never pencil drew'—which can be hoarded and its erotic and
romantic potential savoured in the privacy of the mind's eye:

> One arm aloft— ...
> Holding the bush, to fix it back, she stood,
> A single stream of all her soft brown hair
> Poured on one side: ...
> But the full day dwelt on her brows, and sunned
> Her violet eyes, and all her Hebe bloom,
> And doubled his own warmth against her lips,
> And on the bounteous wave of such a breast
> As never pencil drew ...
>   So home I went, but could not sleep for joy,
> Reading her perfect features in the gloom ...
> And shaping faithful record of the glance
> That graced the giving—
>   (124–74)

In 'The Miller's Daughter' (1832), with guileful
circumstantial precision, the lover-poet positions the girl
'leaning from the [window] ledge above the river', and as in
the development of a daguerreotype, her image forms in the
water's mirror and the poet's gaze:

> And there a vision caught my eye;
>   The reflex of a beauteous form,
>   A glowing arm, a gleaming neck ...
> And when I raised my eyes, above
>   They met with two so full and bright—
> Such eyes!
>   (76–87)

In the oxymoron of the description the eye 'catches' what is
transient, what is in the act of becoming, yet the 'vision' of
the woman is fixed because, as Jennifer Gribble says of the
Lady of Shalott, the woman is 'framed by time and memory,

perpetuating her emblematic significance in the stasis of romantic portraiture' (Gribble 1983; p. 3).

In some poems, the possession is more complete; the woman's consciousness is invaded and, as in ventriloquism, she speaks the man's possession of her and registers the obsessive erotic spell in which she is held. When Fatima says, 'I will . . . Grow, live, die looking on his face, / Die, dying clasped in his embrace' ('Fatima', 40–2), she holds a mirror to the poet-lover's sight which narcissistically reflects his sexual power. Œnone creates a solipsistic world—'I alone awake'—in which all natural objects are held in a stasis mimetic of her erotic dependency on Paris:

> For now the noonday quiet holds the hill:
> The grasshopper is silent in the grass:
> The lizard, with his shadow on the stone,
> Rests like a shadow, and the winds are dead.
> The purple flower droops: the golden bee
> Is lily-cradled: I alone awake.
>
> ('Œnone', 24–9)

Tennyson's contemporary readers responded excitedly to this kind of poetry. Men of varied political and literary inclinations such as W.J. Fox, Arthur Hallam, Christopher North and J.S. Mill shared a sense of the troubling, intriguing qualities of poems like 'The Ballad of Oriana' and 'Mariana' and found them new: 'Words surely never excited a more vivid feeling', wrote Mill, and 'How wonderful the new world thus created for us, the region between real and unreal', said Hallam. For indeed, this was innovative writing. Sweet virtuous girls, luscious Eastern maidens, coquettes, flirts and noble elusive ladies were present in the work of Tennyson's Romantic predecessors, but the poems which mark Tennyson's distinctive quality of writing and which herald the characteristics of his later poetry, poems like 'Mariana', 'Fatima', 'Œnone' and 'The Lady of Shalott', introduce a new type of woman and describe her in a new way. Only Keats had approached the suspenseful sensuality of such poems and his poetry does not achieve the degree of self-conscious eroticism that Tennyson's female impersonations possess. Such female eroticism, or rather the male fantasy of female eroticism which these poems embody, is, as Tennyson's later poems will show, dangerous. Although Mariana is powerless and, like Guinevere after her, given entirely into male keeping for her happiness and her status, she is a threat to male power. It is a function of her passive sexuality to be destructive of the very force—male desire—which creates her. She is the new *femme fatale*.

Yet the source of Mariana's power is essentially domestic and familiar; the 'broken sheds', the buzzing fly, the 'sparrow's chirrup', the poplar tree, these are the appurtenances of everyday life, particularly the enclosed and shuttered lives of middle-class women: 'I am like Mariana in the moated grange', wrote Elizabeth Barrett in 1845, voicing what many women must have felt, 'and sit listening too often to the mouse in the wainscot' (Barrett 1969; I.87). In this ordinariness, Mariana differs from the dangerous women in Romantic poetry who are characterized by beauty which is extraordinary, often unearthly. Mario Praz sees the epitome of this beauty in the Medusa of Shelley's poem:

> ... all the beauty and the terror there—
> A woman's countenance, with serpent-locks,
> Gazing in death on Heaven from those wet rocks.
> ('On the Medusa of Leonardo da Vinci in the
> Florentine Gallery', 38–40)

'This glassy-eyed, severed female head,' says Praz, 'this horrible, fascinating Medusa, was to be the object of the dark loves of the Romantics and the Decadents throughout the whole of the [nineteenth] century' (Praz 1960; p. 43). Yet Praz's prognosis does not fit Tennyson; there are no fatal women of this kind in his poetry. Although there are women who do men harm, none of them has the mystery and terror of Shelley's Medusa or Keat's Belle Dame sans Merci.

'Eleänore' (1832) provides an example of Tennyson's difference in this respect; in a manner that foreshadows the rose-lily dichotomy in *Maud,* the male speaker in this poem makes a dual response to a woman:

In thee all passion becomes passionless,
Touched by thy spirit's mellowness ...
Serene Imperial Eleänore ...

But when I see thee roam, with tresses unconfined,
    ... then, as in a swoon,
With dinning sound my ears are rife,
    My tremulous tongue faltereth,
I lose my colour, I lose my breath,
I drink the cup of a costly death,
Brimmed with delirious draughts of warmest life.
I die with my delight ...

                                        (102–40)

Both Gerhard Joseph and Clyde de L. Ryals have seen
Eleänore as a type of '*the* fatal woman' for Tennyson, a
'powerful figure who traps the minds of all men who gaze on
her'. Joseph sees a development of this response in 'Lady
Clara Vere de Vere' of 1842 where for the first time 'the "I" of
a Tennyson love poem is actively hostile towards such a
woman. . . . After [this] when the fatal woman appears she
does so with increasing virulence' (Joseph 1969; pp. 124–5).

Certainly throughout his career Tennyson's division of
women into good and bad became more pronounced and his
conception of the dangerousness of women intensified and
darkened. But to call his women 'fatal' seems a misnomer
in the context of their Romantic predecessors whose distin-
guishing quality is summarized in Shelley's line: ''Tis the
tempestuous loveliness of terror.' In this line, says Praz,

pleasure and pain are combined in one single impression. The
very objects which should induce a shudder—the livid face of
the severed head, the squirming mass of vipers, the rigidity of
death, the sinister light, the repulsive animals ... all these give
rise to a new sense of beauty, a beauty imperilled and contaminated, a new thrill. (Praz 1960; p. 42)

The Gothic features Praz discovers are not to be found
in Tennyson's dangerous women; even Vivien, the most
obviously wicked of all his women, has none of the terrible
splendour of Shelley's Medusa or the sweet corruption of

Keats's Lamia. In spite of the imagery of snakes and spiders,
Vivien is no more than a coquette:

> And lissome Vivien, holding by his heel,
> Writhed towards him, slided up his knee and sat,
> Behind his ankle twined her hollow feet
> Together, curved an arm about his neck,
> Clung like a snake; and letting her left hand
> Droop from his mighty shoulder as a leaf,
> Made with her right a comb of pearl to part
> The lists of such a beard as youth gone out
> Had left in ashes . . .   drew
> The vast and shaggy mantle of his beard
> Across her neck and bosom to her knee,
> And called herself a gilded summer fly
> Caught in a great old tyrant spider's web,
> Who meant to eat her up in that wild wood
> Without one word.
>   ('Merlin and Vivien', 236–59)

Even though they come from legend and literature,
Tennyson's women have no supernatural power in their
beauty; it does not horrify by its unnaturalness. It is
significant, for example, that Tennyson's interest in the
magic Vivien acquires is perfunctory and that he uses the
thunderstorm as a rather stagy backdrop to the panic-
stricken pleadings of this sexy little gossip and liar rather
than as the magical workings of a real enchantress. Fatal or
otherwise, Vivien and her like are very earth-bound women
who are frequently victims of men's cruelty and neglect, who
suffer from their constrained, dependent positions, and,
most of all, from their own sexual and psychological needs.
Like the fatal women of the Romantics, their danger lies in
the harm they do to men; the difference lies in the kind of
sexuality they possess which is passive, internalized, obsessive, neurotic, but the neurosis of the ordinary woman, or
what the nineteenth century increasingly inclined to think
of as ordinary. If Guinevere and her similarly passionate
and frustrated predecessors have a demonic effect it is
not ostensibly through demonic powers. It is in their

womanliness that the danger lies, not in any fabulous quality. The peril of woman has been transferred from the realms of myth to the drawing-room, has been realized in the social and aesthetic delineaments of the period. The 'serpent-locks' and elfin blood of Shelley and Keats have been transformed into Eleänore's 'large eyes' and 'tresses uncon-fined' or, for that matter, into Vivien's 'vivid smiles, and faintly-venomed points of slander' and Mariana's gasping cry, 'He cometh not'.

Such a sense of the extraordinary power of ordinary female sexuality makes of Tennyson a forceful and early contributor to the explosion of sexual self-consciousness and neurosis characteristic of a period in which, as Michel Foucault has pointed out, it was by no means the case that sex was 'consigned to a shadow existence, but that [the Victorians] dedicated themselves to speaking of it *ad infinitum* while exploiting it as *the* secret' (Foucault 1984; p. 35). Foucault reminds us that:

> Sexuality must not be thought of as a kind of natural given which power tries to hold in check, or as an obscure domain which knowledge tries gradually to uncover. It is the name that can be given to a historical construct: not a furtive reality that is difficult to grasp, but a great surface network in which the stimulation of bodies, the intensification of pleasures, the incitement to discourse, the formation of special knowledges, the strengthening of controls and resistances, are linked to one another, in accordance with a few major strategies of knowledge and power. (ibid. pp. 105–6)

The 'discovery' of Mariana's sexuality, the sexuality of the ordinary woman she represents, is not, then, a discovery of a hidden truth about women; it is rather a 'speaking of' her sexuality as part of a power strategy to do with women but operated by those to whom power is a possessable com-modity, primarily middle-class men. Mariana as women and 'Mariana' as poem are both examples of what Foucault calls 'a hysterization of women's bodies' whereby the female body was 'analysed—qualified and disqualified—as being thoroughly saturated with sexuality . . . integrated into the sphere of medical practice [and] placed in organic communication with the social body, the family and the life of children' (ibid. p. 104). Whilst certainly previously, in the eighteenth century for example, women were categorized in relation to men, as wife, daughter, widow, and so on, in the nineteenth century this increasingly becomes not merely an economic and legal classification but also a 'hysterical' one. Woman's function and image becomes defined by her sexuality, literally, by the possession of a womb (hystera), and the state of her womb—virgin, senile, replete, menstruating, privately or communally owned—becomes her categorized biological, and even pathological, state of being female. In social terms the state is translated into the recognizable types of the Victorian literacy scene: pure maiden, 'redundant' woman, Madonna and matron, invalid and neurotic, sensualist and fallen woman. Any of Dickens's novels can supply examples of all such types.

Mariana is herself the type of the lovelorn, waiting woman, but she is also more than that. As Millais recognized in his 1857 painting of the poem and as Elizabeth Barrett also sensed when she compared her imprisoned and undecided state to Mariana's, in the suspended and incomplete, and therefore provocative, nature of her predicament Mariana invokes all the other types of woman with which Victorian ideology will be concerned, an ominous and seductive questioner of the fate of womankind: will Angelo deliver her into marriage, will she grow old alone, will she go mad or onto the streets, or will she die as she says she wishes to? Even now, and certainly in 1830 when the poem was written, the problem the poem leaves with its readers is what to do with Mariana's nubility, how to assuage her desperate sexuality. In the Victorian sexual economy, Mariana's 'development' must take place in one of three ways: in motherhood, in prostitution and, as the only alternative to these polarities, in death. Each of these bears a negative and a positive aspect: the good or the bad mother; the prostitute who is a creature of shame and disease or an instrument of redemption; the woman who dies in spiritual and sexual purity or who withers into sterility and hagdom. The link between all three categories is, of course, the instatement of masculinity and the upholding of male power.

CHAPTER SEVEN

The Mother

Is this an allegory? If not, Ida is most unjustifiably disagreeable. (Coventry Patmore's pencilled comment in his copy of *The Princess*)

For a man to assume manhood he must cease to be overtly dependent on and controlled by his mother because such dependency marked his condition as a helpless infant. Moreover, he sees that, in the adult world to which he normally aspires, men have control over women. As an individual man grows into consciousness of his maleness he must inevitably proceed, as Erich Neumann describes it,

> to deny the genetic principle, which is precisely the basic principle of the matriarchal world. Or, mythologically speaking, he murders his mother and undertakes the patriarchal revaluation by which the son identified with the father makes himself the source from which the Feminine—like Eve arising from Adam's rib—originates in a spiritual and antinatural way. (Neumann 1972; p. 58)

Tennyson 'conceives' his mothers in two contrasting ways which conform to notions of good and bad but which are each concerned with negation of the mother, either through her infantilization or through her conquest and transformation into the ideal Feminine.

The image of the good mother appears in only a few of Tennyson's poems; she is characterized by the passive

110

virtues—chastity, humility and obedience—and her strengths
are those of sympathy, gentleness and endurance: 'The
summer calm of golden charity . . . A courage to endure and
to obey' ('Isabel', 8,25). In appearance she is modest—'locks
not wide-spread, / Madonna-wise on either side her head' (5–
6)—and her eyes, particularly, are devout and tender: 'Thy
mild deep eyes . . . that knew / The beauty and repose of
faith, / And the clear spirit shining through' ('Supposed
Confessions', 74–6). Such mothers influence their sons and
husbands through pious precept and example, a responsibility
women ought to feel keenly, as Sarah Stickney Ellis, writing
in 1839, made clear:

> How often has man returned to his home with a mind confused
> by the many voices, which in the mart, the exchange, or the
> public assembly, have addressed themselves to his inborn
> selfishness, or his worldly pride; and while his integrity was
> shaken, and his resolution gave way beneath the pressure of
> apparent necessity, or the insidious pretences of expediency, he
> has stood corrected before the clear eye of woman, as it looked
> directly to the naked truth, and detected the lurking evil of the
> specious act he was about to commit. . . . He has thought of the
> humble monitress who sat alone, guarding the fireside comforts
> of his distant home; and the remembrance of her character,
> clothed in moral beauty, has scattered the clouds before his
> mental vision, and sent him back to that beloved home, a wiser
> and a better man. (Ellis 1839; pp. 72–3)

This is echoed in *The Princess* in the Prince's acclaim of his
mother:

>   . . . all male minds perforce
> Swayed to her from their orbits as they moved
> And girdled her with music. Happy he
> With such a mother! . . .
> . . . trust in all things high
> Comes easy to him, and though he trip and fall
> He shall not blind his soul with clay.
>   (VII.306–12)

This kind of maternal influence over the adult man develops
from maternal solicitude for him as an infant:

Thrice happy state again to be
The trustful infant on the knee!
Who lets his rosy fingers play
About his mother's neck, and knows
Nothing beyond his mother's eyes.
They comfort him by night and day; . . .
Oh! sure it is a special care . . .
      ('Supposed Confessions' 40–63)

On the basis of these quotations, women's power would seem
to be great. Yet because it is a relative power, operative only
as nurture or support for the son, it should never be equal to
or complete with him. This requires the relegation of
mothers either to a nostalgic past which death has idealized,
like the mother in 'Supposed Confessions' and the mother
'so gentle and good' of the hero of *Maud*, or her infantilization
as a 'natural' to whom learning and moral and intellectual
sophistication are alien. The Prince's mother in *The Princess*
is described as 'whole and one', 'as whole as some serene /
Creation minted in the golden moods / Of sovereign artists'
(V.185–7), and this notion of a woman as simple and
uncomplex and perhaps also a simpleton complements that
of the more variable, extreme and self-conscious moral life of
a man, the 'piebald miscellany . . . Bursts of great heart and
slips in sensual mire' (V.190–1). The inference is that
women are good unconsciously, by virtue of what Ruskin in
1863 called a 'majestic childishness' (and Tennyson referred
to as 'childlike'); not for them the truly human struggle with
right and wrong, spirit and flesh, but an intuitive, indeed
instinctive, existence as the objects of men's sentimental
veneration and contempt. Women are trapped within their
maternal function, a biological imperative which unless
thwarted renders them tender, good and stupid. It is for this
reason that Tennyson emphasized the child in *The Princess*
which he said was 'the link through the parts, as shown in the
Songs . . . which are the best interpreters of the poem'. The
moment of Psyche's reunion with her child, when her breast
responds instinctively to its needs—'half / The sacred
mother's bosom, panting, burst / The laces toward her babe'
(VI.131–3)—provides a lesson which not even Ida can

ignore. As Cyril says, 'Love and Nature, these are two more
terrible and stronger' in their instinctive demands than the
intellectual and moral claims of Ida's case. Psyche's banish-
ment—'I go to mine own land / For ever . . . I scarce am fit for
your great plans'—enacts for all women their relegation to
the domestic sphere, to the silenced and passive side of that
division between public and private life which their maternal
function creates.

The imaginative impoverishment of Tennyson's notion of
the good mother is illustrated in the strained pictorialism of
his description of Psyche's appearance at the reunion with
her child:

> wan was her cheek
> With hollow watch, her blooming mantle torn,
> Red grief and mother's hunger in her eye,
> And down dead-heavy sank her curls, and half
> The sacred mother's bosom, panting, burst
> The laces toward her babe;
> (VI.128–33)

It is as though Tennyson has in mind a Renaissance painting,
or a Victorian imitation of one such as Etty or Leighton
might have done, the kind of picture in which the subject
matter—motherhood, the 'sacred ... bosom' of a bare-
breasted madonna—licences a timid and slightly fatigued
pornographic treatment.

The artificiality of the description, and its perfunctory
reliance on the traditions of religious iconography, are in
contrast to Tennyson's poignant and considered—and his
final—treatment of the conception of the good woman as
yielding breast in a late poem, 'Demeter and Persephone'
(1889). Here Demeter, whom Tennyson 'considered one of
the most beautiful types of womanhood', recalls her loss of
Persephone to Aïdoneus, the God of Death; in her anguish
of motherhood Demeter succours and pities the whole
world:

> [I] went in search of thee
> Through many a palace, many a cot, and gave

Thy breast to ailing infants in the night,
And set the mother waking in amaze
To find her sick one whole; and forth again
Among the wail of midnight winds, and cried,
'Where is my loved one? Wherefore do ye wail?'
And out from all the night an answer shrilled,
'We know not, and we know not why we wail.' ...
I thridded the black heart of all the woods,
I peered through tomb and cave, and in the storms
Of Autumn swept across the city, and heard
The murmur of their temples chanting me
Me, me, the desolate Mother! 'Where'?—and
    turned,
And fled by many a waste, forlorn of man,
And grieved for man through all my grief for thee ...
                                        (53–74)

Written in old age, this is a poem which yearns for Demeter's
maternal compassion and regeneration and accredits her
with a vision of a new religion of love:

                                        Gods,
To quench, not hurl the thunderbolt, to stay,
Not spread the plague, the famine; Gods indeed,
To send the noon into the night and break
The sunless halls of Hades into Heaven?
                                        (130–4)

But the kind of unproblematic mother-figure that Demeter
represents is rare in Tennyson's poetry, a pious hope rather
than a realized presence. As I hope to show in Chapter 10 in
regard to *In Memoriam*, the *relationship* of the protagonist to
the maternal function is a haunting and evocative subtext in
the poem, but on an overtly thematic level, mother-love in
Tennyson is overshadowed by or easily transforms itself into
a figure in marked contrast to Demeter. Such a figure Erich
Neumann calls the Terrible Mother who devours her
children, who disobeys nature or, perhaps more fearsomely,
follows a contrary, anarchic principle in nature which is
unfavourable to the development of a supremacist order of
male succession. This is the mother who must be vanquished

by the son if he is to attain manhood. Indeed, the conflict may be necessary to that attainment, as Neumann says:

> Her appearance may introduce a positive development in which the ego is driven toward masculinization and the fight with the dragon, that is, positive development and transformation . . . the myth of Perseus is typical: Perseus must kill the Terrible Mother before he can win Andromeda. (Neumann 1972; p. 45)

In 'Motherhood According to Bellini', Julia Kristeva describes a painting in which the maternal presence is threatening and dragonish rather than comforting:

> Aggressive hands prod the stomach and penis of the frightened baby who . . . frees himself violently, taking his mother's hands along on his body. All the while, the folds of the virginal gown separate this little dramatic theater from the maternal body, whose illuminated face alone is revealed. Her characterless gaze fleeting under her downcast eyelids, the nonetheless definite pleasure, unshakable in its intimacy, and her cheeks radiating peace, all constitute a strange modesty. (Kristeva 1980; p. 254)

These are the delineaments of the Terrible Mother whose pleasure lies elsewhere than in her baby and whose relation with him seems to be not the passive one of adoration but the active one of sexual molestation. Tennyson's poems are not Bellini paintings but nevertheless they too register an anxiety about women whose attention and desire lie beyond the men who claim them, and whose indifference, if not their actual aggression, is a castration threat which must be averted if the male is to survive and dominate.

The Princess is a comic and somewhat bare-faced treatment of this theme. Ida, of course, is not literally a mother, but in her proud isolation and independence she represents unaccommodated woman, in psychoanalytic terms, the phallic mother of the poet-lover's pre-Oedipal phase, who is both exciting and terrifying and whose dark secret place must be invaded and violated. The Prince and his companions do this by becoming babies again: they wear frocks, just as little Victorian boys did, and their journey is through 'the lean and wrinkled precipes, / By every coppice-feathered chasm and cleft, / Drop[ping] through ambrosial gloom' (IV.4–6). They return, as it were, to the moment of birth when their identity bursts upon the group of women and Ida is swept into the flood, 'the horrible fall'. Her delivery from this, by the Prince, ensures this time her right development into the nurturing mother whose whole attention is directed toward her son-lover. His own rebirth from early effeminacy into manhood can only be accomplished by her adoration; like a Madonna and Child, not one of Bellini's fraught pairings but one perhaps by Botticelli or Raphael, they now gaze upon each other:

> palm to palm she sat: the dew
> Dwelt in her eyes, and softer all her shape
> And rounder seemed: I moved: I sighed: a touch
> Came round my wrist, and tears upon my hand:
> . . . and with what life I had,
> And like a flower that cannot all unfold,
> So drenched it is with tempest, to the sun,
> Yet, as it may, turns toward him, I on her
> Fixt my faint eyes . . .
>
> (VII.120–9)

When Tennyson said of *The Princess* that 'the child is the link through the parts', he was referring to Aglaïa, Psyche's baby, who softens Ida's heart, and to woman's responsibility to 'stay . . . all the fair young planet in her hands'. But the child is also the adult man, man as baby, and what is important is his relationship with the mothers in the poem. For this is a much be-mothered poem—Psyche, Blanche, the dead mothers of the Prince and Ida—and the Prince knows that Ida's threat to transform the category, far beyond even Blanche's embittered version, if successful, will turn all the company of women into dragons rather than Andromedas or Demeters. Ida, perhaps, comes nearest of all Tennyson's dangerous women to the *femme fatale* of monstrous properties that the Romantics celebrated. The idea of her proposed in the Prologue is of 'some great Princess, six feet high, / Grand, epic, homicidal' (218–9), and although this is modified in the main story, vestiges remain in her height, her tame leopards and her imperiousness, and in the many masculine features she displays, a masculinity still vestigially present in the image, quoted above, of her as the sun to whom the drenched flower turns. With something like wonder at this doomed creature of his imagination, whose power at this point in the poem, before her reclamation into the orthodox femininity of patriarchy, can only be given in male terms, Tennyson describes her journey with her women after the battle and before her capitulation to the Prince:

> so they came: anon
> Through open field into the lists they wound
> Timorously; and as the leader of the herd
> That holds a stately fretwork to the Sun,
> And followed up by a hundred airy does,
> Steps with such a tender foot, light as on air,
> The lovely, lordly creature floated on
> To where her wounded brethren lay;
> 						(VI.67–74)

The fate of Ida, in which her dangers and attractions are registered only to be tamed and domesticated, is magnified in the treatment of Lilia, Ida's modern counterpart who sets Ida's story in motion and whose aspirations are the threatening voice of nineteenth-century feminism which *The Princess* aims to contain and neutralize. In Lilia the 'great Princess' is reduced to the little sister, the 'little hearth-flower Lilia', who can be affectionately patronized and whose protest on behalf of the 'thousands now / Such women' can be dispelled within the ideology of romantic sentiment:

> At this upon the sward
> She tapt her tiny silken-sandaled foot:
> 'That's your light way; but I would make it death
> For any male thing but to peep at us.'

> Petulant she spoke, and at herself she laughed;
> A rosebud set with little wilful thorns,
> And sweet as English air could make her, she;
> 						(Prol. 148–54)

The incongruity here between Lilia's death threat (which is magnified in Ida's injunction LET NO MAN ENTER IN ON PAIN OF DEATH (II.178)) and the requisite infantilisms of Victorian girlhood (the 'tiny silken-sandaled foot' and the vocabulary of coquetry—'petulant', 'wilful', 'rosebud', 'sweet') raises the question of Lilia's future, particularly in the light of her feminism. Ideally, as in Ida's case, this will be accommodated within marriage but if Lilia resists this, the poem offers her two alternatives, or rather one alternative, Aunt Elizabeth, and the exaggerated version of this maiden aunt in Lady Blanche. Both these middle-aged women are feminists; Aunt Elizabeth is also something of a socialist: '[she] preached / An universal culture for the crowd, / And all things great' (Introd. 108–10). Her danger to men and the marriage institution is that she is knowledgeable and loquacious and that she may have the answer to 'what we [women] are' (Concl. 34) but this danger is not great because it can be seen as the utterance of one of the 'redundant' women of the period; 'she was crammed with theories out of books' (Concl. 35) suggests the compensatory nature of her wisdom. In Lady Blanche, however, the danger is more anxiously and therefore more misogynistically registered. Lady Blanche has almost corrupted Ida and is bent on doing the same to Melissa but for the timely intervention of Florian, and the enormity of these attempted acts of indirect castration of men is signalled in the text by Blanche's spitefulness, her ugliness, and, most of all, her age: 'Lady Blanche ... Of faded form and haughtiest lineaments, / With all her autumn tresses falsely brown' (II.424–6); '[she] stretched a vulture throat, / And shot from crooked lips a haggard smile' (IV.344–5). Cyril's efforts to pacify her are given in the terms of a contemptuous rape:

> Hither came
> Cyril, and yawning 'O hard task,' he cried;
> 'No fighting shadows here! I forced a way
> Through solid opposition crabbed and gnarled.
> Better to clear prime forests, heave and thump
> A league of street in summer solstice down,
> Than hammer at this reverend gentlewoman.
>   (III.107–13)

This is the threatened punishment of a modern-day witch, of a woman who places herself beyond what patriarchy considers safe and useful: neither young nor beautiful, no longer a bearer of children or a sexual object, Blanche dangerously compounds the superfluity of her existence by her radical feminism which converts Aunt Elizabeth's theories into separatist practice.

In an important sense, *The Princess* is very simply a moral lesson for Lilia and all the young women of England like her; it is a lesson to which, however weighted with special pleading, Tennyson is just honest and serious enough as a poet to make Lilia respond ambiguously: 'the sequel of the tale / Had touched her; and she sat, she plucked the grass, / She flung it from her, thinking' (Concl. 31–2). The alternatives for her future the poem offers are narrowed down to marriage—or the tedious irrelevance of Aunt Elizabeth or the monstrous hagdom of Blanche. Tennyson's investment in Lilia's choosing correctly is suggested in his inclusion of the figure of Lilia's father:

> And there we saw Sir Walter where he stood,
> Before a tower of crimson holly-hoaks,
> Among six boys, head under head, and looked
> No little lily-handed Baronet he,
> A great broad-shouldered genial Englishman,
> A lord of fat prize-oxen and of sheep ...
> A pamphleteer on guano and on grain,
> A quarter-sessions chairman, abler none;
>   (Concl. 81–90)

On Sir Walter's prosperity and landed succession, and his enlightened control of and popularity amongst the masses, depends the progressive conservatism Tennyson valued. And in turn, what Sir Walter depends on is—Lilia; unless she conforms to her traditional role in patriarchy as the transmitter of property and the legitimizer of sexual energy, in short, as the mother of 'six boys', the system will fall.

Tennyson's awareness of the centrality of Lilia to the scheme of things, a centrality he will affirm with increasing vehemence throughout his poetry, is made clear in his

linkage of 'revolts, republics, revolutions' (Concl. 65) with
the comic-solemn story of 'our wild Princess' (69). Yet it is a
contradiction, and an embarrassing one at that, to admit that
the absurdity of women's rights is a deadly serious issue, is
'something real'; it is 'to wrestle with a burlesque', and
Tennyson's unease both with the situation itself and his own
position 'betwixt the mockers and the realists' is registered in
his sliding away from the issues he raises in what he aptly
describes as a 'strange diagonal'. The questioning and
unresolved nature of the poem, and particularly of Lilia's
destiny, is indicated in the ambivalence of the final lines
of the poem where Lilia 'rising quietly / Disrobed the
glimmering statue of Sir Ralph / From those rich silks'.

CHAPTER EIGHT

The Fallen Woman

> in the entire history of patrilineal or class-stratified
> societies, it is the lot of the feminine to assume the role of *waste,*
> or of the hidden work-force in the relationships of production
> and the language which defines them. (Julia Kristeva, *About
> Chinese Women)*

Although her future constitutes the debate of *The Princess*,
at the end of the poem Lilia is still the pure lily, the sweet
little sister of men's fond imaginings, the kind of girl
Lancelot has in mind when he dreams of the 'maiden Saint
who stands with lily in hand' ('Balin and Balan', 256). But
Guinevere reminds him of the opposite of this: '"Sweeter to
me" she said "this garden-rose / Deep-hued and many-
folded"' (264–5), and at this reminder of female sexuality
Lancelot is once more 'Deep-tranced' in his obsession with
her. Guinevere is 'fairest of all flesh' and 'all earth's beauty'
and this 'rose' rather than 'lily' quality in her is the flaw in
Arthur's scheme because it enthralls the noblest of his
knights, Lancelot, and brings the moral collapse of all those
who emulate him. Better for Camelot would have been the
kind of woman Tennyson described in an early poem, 'Amy':

> ... starry countenance
> Wherein I lose myself from life, and wander
> In utter ignorance
> As in some other world where strong desire
> Fulfils ideals and draws .

Homeward to all things men of orders higher
Subject to loftier laws.

(58–64)

Guinevere's crime is not that she is deliberately destructive,
as Vivien is, but that she is desirous as well as desirable. Her
beauty is unproblematic whilst it remains the passive
possession of her owner, Arthur, but when it becomes
energized by wayward sexual longing for another man, it not
only deprives Arthur of his possession but nullifies Lancelot
too. Uncontrolled, unlegalized female sexual desire both
emasculates men and reduces their manly function; Arthur's
'vast design and purpose' is broken and Lancelot's 'own name
shames [him], seeming a reproach'; both men die heirless.
Equally, Guinevere is a victim of her own sexuality; once
awakened, 'imprinted', by Lancelot she is trapped in her
'false voluptuous pride', and because female sexual desire is
incompatible with moral self-consciousness she sinks to an
instinctual level, taking 'full easily all impressions from
below'. In Guinevere, Mariana's desire, uncontrolled and
misdirected, exacts its fearful toll in the figure of the
adulterous wife.

'Guinevere', published in 1859, is an uncompromising
statement on the power of female sexuality to bring down a
state. When Arthur says to Guinevere, 'mine own flesh, /
Here looking down on thine polluted, cries / "I loathe thee"'
('Guinevere', 551–3), he seems to speak of a revulsion which
is Tennyson's as well as his own. Such revulsion is an
intensification of an unease with women's power registered
in the early poems. In 'Eleänore' (1831), for instance, the
protagonist loses colour and breath and 'drink[s] the cup of a
costly death' at the woman's attractions; by 1837, in the lyric
'O that 'twere possible' (which later provided the 'germ' of
Maud) this unease has become a darker response and the
good aspects of love are accompanied by shadowy figures of
shame and guilt:

Through the hubbub of the market
I steal, a wasted frame;

It crosseth here, it crosseth there—
Through all that crowd, confused and loud,
   The shadow still the same;
And on my heavy eyelids
   My anguish hangs like shame.
                           (42–8)

In Tennyson's use of this lyric in *Maud* (1855), which was
his first long poem as Poet Laureate, the perception of sexual
love as tortured and mysterious comes to occupy a central
position. In the context of the protagonist's ravings about the
commercial evils of his society, the shadowy figures take on
the aspects of inhabitants of an industrial landscape of fog,
noise, squalor and poverty, an urban wasteland in which the
protagonist is importuned by loveless faces. As in Eliot's
poem, this is the wasteland of prostitution and all women,
unless they are the hyacinth girl, are implicated in its dark
practices:

   But the broad light glares and beats,
   And the shadow flits and fleets
   And will not let me be;
   And I loathe the squares and streets,
   And the faces that one meets,
   Hearts with no love for me:
              (*Maud* II.229–34)

The dichotomy between the erotic and non-erotic responses
to women, mildly registered in 'Eleänore', has by the time of
Maud become dramatically intensified. The result is a
slippage in which not just sexual transgression by women but
even desire for them becomes contaminated and transformed
into licentiousness. Desire, it seems, is tainted, and although
Tennyson's attitude to women is not quite that of King
Pellam who would let no 'dame or damsel enter at his gates /
Lest he should be polluted' ('Balin and Balan', 104–5), the
pollution of women, once they have fallen from their angelic
role, is an inevitable consequence and is perceived as a
deceptive sickness which 'creeps . . . among the crowd . . .
saps / The fealty of our friends, and stirs the pulse / With

devil's leaps, and poisons half the young' ('Guinevere', 516–19).

What Tennyson has in mind here is, of course, venereal disease, both as a weakener of manhood and as a congenital infection. Prostitutes, adulteresses, and perhaps potentially all women are the source of a corruption which can destroy a nation; Guinevere is no prostitute but her defection from absolute standards of purity draws her into complicity with a dark and ruinous sisterhood of fallen women whom mid-Victorian England believed were undermining the social structure. As Keith Nield has explained, 'for thirty years from the late 1850s, female prostitution was widely treated as a problem of major social concern. . . . There were many at the time who came to share with the "Times" [of 6 May 1857] a view of prostitution as the "Greatest of our Social Evils"' (Nield 1973; Introd.). In blaming Guinevere for the fall of Camelot Tennyson was voicing anxieties prevalent at the time the poem was written and during the next two decades or so, as William Acton realized when he incorporated the lines just quoted from 'Guinevere' in the second edition (1870) of his by now famous work *Prostitution*. Acton's context to the quotation concerns the nature of an unchaste woman, the true prostitute of gross appetites not the mere unfortunates whom poverty reduces to prostitution:

> She is a woman with half the woman gone, and that half containing all that elevates her nature, leaving her a mere instrument of impurity . . . a social pest, carrying contamination and foulness to every quarter to which she has access, who,
> like a . . . disease . . .
> Creeps, no precaution used, among the crowd,
> Makes wicket lightnings of her eyes, . . .
> . . . and stirs the pulse,
> With devil's leaps, and poisons half the young.
> Such women, ministers of evil passions, not only gratify desire, but also arouse it . . . and suggest evil thoughts which might otherwise remain undeveloped . . . thousands would remain uncontaminated if temptation did not seek them out. (Acton 1968; p. 119)

It is significant that not only the Tennyson quotation but the whole of this passage is an addition to the second edition of *Prostitution*, and that it is more heated and condemnatory than anything in the first edition. Of course, Acton wrote in the first instance for other medical men, whereas the second edition was a popularization of a work which had become surprisingly well known and which, along with the same author's *The Functions and Disorders of the Reproductive Organs* (also 1857, reaching its third edition by 1862), seemed to hit the note of the age. Nevertheless, the difference between the first and second editions of *Prostitution* is striking evidence of a rising panic and revulsion in connection with prostitution, venereal disease, and sexual irregularity in general, a tide of feeling in which Tennyson played a not unimportant part in his polarization of women into saints and sinners through the publication of 'Guinevere' and 'Vivien', along with 'Elaine' and 'Enid', in 1859. In a sense Tennyson and Acton can be seen as locked together in a spiral of indignation which represents both cause and symptom of the feeling of the times. Tennyson would certainly have read Acton, or reviews of his book, in or soon after 1857 and this literature would have stimulated by its scientific evidence his already existing sense of the pollution women cause. In his turn, Acton introduced into his medical work a condemnation which he 'authorized' by quoting the Poet Laureate in the manner we have seen. And so onwards, in an escalation of fascinated horror, which expressed itself in the exaggeration of the number of prostitutes, in the explosion of sensationalist discourse on the topic, and in the eventual attempts to exert legal control by various Acts of Parliament culminating in the Contagious Diseases Acts of 1864, 1866 and 1869. But as history has shown, prostitution was no new problem, and at some periods of history it has not been seen as particularly a problem at all. Why should it become *the* social problem at this time? Increased urbanization may have raised the numbers and visibility of prostitutes but not to the extent claimed and not in proportion to the outcry the topic created. Nield suggests that prostitutes, who were mostly working-class women, lived

and worked 'in the subculture of chronic urban poverty and
petty criminality ... a world of overcrowded housing and
blighted expectations of work and wages. 'At these levels', he
maintains, prostitution was 'a part of the collective life of the
urban poor' (Nield 1973; Introd.) and therefore came to
represent a problem larger than itself, a focus for middle-
class fears about worsening urban conditions and the 'socially
corrosive character', and even revolutionary potential, of the
lumpenproletariat. Yet although the fears were real enough,
speaking about them, whether in scandalized journalism,
pious tract, medical treatise, pornography or Laureate
poetry, became a compulsive occupation. In Foucault's
terms, prostitution becomes a secret which is spoken of *ad
infinitum* and its 'promotion' and control become both a
means by which class and sexual mores and divisions could
be constructed and consolidated, and also a strategy for
policing society and disciplining its members.

Tennyson's 'Lucretius' (1868) illustrates how the prostitute (or the loose woman, the amorous women, or, indeed,
the ordinary, imperfect woman; by this time there is a
curious conflation of all these on the dark side of his
dichotomy of women) provides one of the 'especially dense
transfer points' (Foucault 1984; p. 103) in a discourse in
which a power structure and a value hierarchy is being
established and endorsed. Tennyson composed this poem,
which is a microcosmic version of *Idylls of the King* in that it
charts the collapse of rationality and sanity in a man through
the action of a woman, shortly after the publication of a full-
scale edition of the Roman poet Lucretius by Hugh Monroe
in 1864. Lucretius was obviously a poet to appeal to the
nineteenth century: a scientist, perhaps even a positivist,
who viewed nature as an evolutionary force, a materialist
philosopher who nevertheless found sublimity and awe in
the nature of things, he would have seemed to the Victorians
a type of thinker such as their own period produced in men
like T.H. Huxley or J.S. Mill, a vindication of human
rationality. His long poem *De Rerum Natura* is a hymn
of praise to Epicurus as a liberator of humanity from
superstition and the fear of the unknown, and the poem

itself is evidence of an unusually purposeful and powerful intellect.

Tennyson's poem is constructed by the adaptation of passages from Lucretius's work, but framed and structured by the legend (for which there is no support in classical sources) concerning his death, which was that he went mad and committed suicide after being given a love potion, possibly by his wife, Lucilia. Tennyson probably read of the legend in his boyhood. 'Lucretius' is, then, a poem about madness, the unhinging of a great mind by a woman who, in Tennyson's telling of the legend, is not wicked, not a Vivien, but neglected and amorous, Mariana driven to desperate means. Furthermore, not only is Lucilia guilty of provoking the madness, but the madness itself is chiefly manifested in visions of depraved or licentious female sexuality:

> ... girls, Hetairai, curious in their art,
> Hired animalisms ...
> ... —and worst disease of all,
> These prodigies of myriad nakednesses,
> And twisted shapes of lust, unspeakable,
> Abominable, strangers at my hearth
> Not welcome, harpies miring every dish,
> The phantom husks of something foully done ...
> (52–3; 155–60)

Such violent passages are not from Lucretius but are Tennyson's additions, his attempt to delineate and explain madness, a topic always of intense concern to him. More than this, it is as though all the great anxieties of the Victorian period, as well as of Tennyson's own intellectual and emotional life, concerning nature, science, art, religion and the life of the individual are focused on this figure of an importunate woman. 'Wrathful and petulant', her demonic import is unmistakably visible in the trajectory of the poem from its domestic beginning through Lucretius's ravings and philosophizings to his suicide. Although there is no logical connection between Lucilia and the 'atom and void, atom and void' of Lucretius's final vision, there is no doubt of the emotional link between her unassuaged sexuality and his destruction.

The opening section of this poem is a clear statement of the
'twy-natured' universe Tennyson now inhabits in which
women represent and appeal to the lower half, that which lies
beneath and which threatens to disrupt the rationalist ethic
that Tennyson, through Lucretius, seeks to protect:

> Lucilia, wedded to Lucretius, found
> Her master cold; for when the morning flush
> Of passion and the first embrace had died
> Between them, though he loved her none the less,
> Yet often when the woman heard his foot
> Return from pacings in the field, and ran
> To greet him with a kiss, the master took
> Small notice, or austerely, for—his mind
> Half buried in some weightier argument,
> Or fancy-borne perhaps upon the rise
> And long roll of the Hexameter—he past
> To turn and ponder those three hundred scrolls
> Left by the Teacher, whom he held divine.
> She brooked it not; but wrathful, petulant,
> Dreaming some rival, sought and found a witch
> Who brewed the philtre which had power, they said,
> To lead an errant passion home again.
> And this, at times, she mingled with his drink,
> And this destroyed him; for the wicked broth
> Confused the chemic labour of the blood,
> And tickling the brute brain within the man's
> Made havock among those tender cells, and checked
> His power to shape: he loathed himself;
>
> (1–23)

Here poetry and philosophy, and all the higher operations
of the mind, belong to a male tradition—Epicurus ('the
Teacher'), Lucretius and, necessarily, Tennyson—which
excludes women. Good women within patriarchy accept the
exclusion, like the wife in section XCVII of *In Memoriam*
('She darkly feels him great and wise, / She dwells on him
with faithful eyes, / "I cannot understand: I love."') whom
Eleanor Marx described as 'that objectionable product of
capitalism' (Marx and Aveling 1886; p. 221). The damage
done by a woman of Lucilia's kind is in the destruction of

man's illusion of distance from himself, from his own body and his animal inheritance; in 'tickling the brute brain within the man's' she returns him to a wholeness in which the 'long roll of the Hexameter' would be one with, for example, giving birth, or any physical imperative belonging to a Nature over which the mastery cannot be guaranteed. As the poem makes clear, the Hexameter, the 'three hundred scrolls / Left by the Teacher', Lucretius's own 'golden work', present a more convincing illusion of control over flux and time than the palpably changeful alternative offered by nature, the flesh, the sexual impulse and, of course, woman, who is in league with all of these: 'death, and palsy, death-in-life, / And wretched age—and worse disease of all, / These prodigies of myriad nakedness' (154–6). In writing of prostitution in 1850, W.R. Greg had indicated the precarious balance a man must keep in his sexual relations between fornication and love; his discussion implies that each is an animal activity, to do with nature, but in love 'the higher organization of man enables him to elevate and refine [it]' whereas fornication 'brings man down to a level with the brutes' (quoted Nield 1973; p. 450) and in some respects lower than brutes. Virility may be necessary to a 'man's consciousness of his dignity, of his character as head and ruler, and of his importance', but virile activity, the basic physiological urgings of desire and the act of coition, was alarmingly vulnerable to connotations of bestiality unless a man could be inspired to elevate and refine it. There is little wonder that woman was blamed for man's dilemma, and that she became both cause and metonymic representation of his mortal dissatisfactions.

'Lucretius' was published in 1868, shortly before 'The Holy Grail' and 'Pelleas and Ettarre'. Grouped together, the poems of the period around 1870 show Tennyson acutely concerned with the dangers of sexual licence. As Robert Martin says, 'He had always been conservative, even prudish, in his attitudes to sex ... but now he seemed to smell it out everwhere.' Martin continues: 'there is no evidence of anything specific in his life or that of his family to account for this morbid concern', which he suggests derived from

Tennyson's religious anxieties and 'the old duality of spirit
and matter that had perplexed him for so long' (Martin 1980;
pp. 481–2). Exacerbating factors included the passing of the
Reform Bill of 1867, which in its enfranchisement of a
section of the working classes increased Tennyson's fear
of social breakdown, and, perhaps most important, the
growing impact of Darwinism. The only mention of Darwin
in the biography of Tennyson by his son is for the year 1868
when Emily recorded in her journal a visit Darwin made to
Farringford in August of that year: 'Mr. Darwin called, and
seemed to be very kindly, unworldly, and agreeable. A. said
to him, "Your theory of Evolution does not make against
Christianity": and Darwin answered "No, certainly not"'
(Tennyson 1897; II.57). However much credence Tennyson
may have given to Darwin's reply, the fact that he asked the
question at all points to his sense of nature's unreliability
as testimony to divine purposes. Never the source of
unsullied inspiration it had been for some of his Romantic
predecessors, nature has become for Tennyson a deeply
treacherous survivalist force. And, of course, nature is
feminine, Nature as mother and whore, forever involving
man in her incalculable and unstable practices: 'with how
great ease Nature can smile, / Balmier and nobler from her
bath of storm, / At random savage' ('Lucretius', 174–6). The
personification of Nature as female, first present to a
noticeable degree in *In Memoriam* and persistent in *Maud*,
now attains almost hysterical levels in 'Lucretius' and the
confrontation with her becomes crucial in that most Darwinian
of poems.

The crux of 'Lucretius' is the impossibility of holding to a
belief in absolute divinity given an atomistic universe:

> The Gods, the Gods!
> If all be atoms, how then should the Gods
> Being atomic not be dissoluble,
> Not follow the great law?
>
>   (113–16)

Involved in this dilemma is not merely the question of the
purpose of human life but also the more serious ontological

problem of identity and subjectivity. Human selfhood and the concept of a centred selfhood of the Gods are interdependent; when one dissolves, the other dissolves too:

> [I] . . . meant
> Surely to lead . . .
> . . . onward to the proof
> That Gods there are, and deathless. Meant? I meant?
> I have forgotten what I meant: my mind
> Stumbles, and all my faculties are lamed.
>
> (118–23)

What causes the dissolution is Lucilia, but Lucilia is really no more than the instrument of an even more powerful female force, Nature. Although nature can be a mother—'the all-generating powers and genial heat / Of Nature, when . . . lambs are glad / Nosing the mother's udder' (97–100)—, wherein she fulfls her role in patriarchal metaphysics of making 'things appear the work of mighty Gods', this fecundity is but one aspect of a promiscuous flux which threatens male control and male meaning. As the greatest whore of all, she is the wastage in men's lives; she resists fixity and boundary, she is the 'flaming atom-steams / And torrents of [a] myriad universe' (38–9), she is the void that engulfs male selfhood. Philosophy, science, poetry, the 'settled sweet Epicurean life', all this, as Lucretius says, 'breaks / As I am breaking now! [into] the womb and tomb of all, / Great Nature' (241–4).

Lucretius's suicide speech—'O Thou, / Passionless bride, divine Tranquillity, / Yearned after by the wisest of the wise. . ., (264–6)—contains, as Christopher Ricks has pointed out (Ricks 1969; p. 1217), an adaptation of a line (quoted above p. 18) from one of Tennyson's very earliest poems, *The Devil and the Lady*. In that juvenile work, it is Nature who speaks wisely to the 'passionless tranquillity' of boyhood. In the intervening forty-five years, this idea, these words, have broodingly shifted their base; now tranquillity is sought not in Nature but in escape from her in nihilism: 'Thus—thus: the soul flies out and dies in the air' (273).

CHAPTER NINE

Women and Death

Any man has to, needs to, wants to
Once in a lifetime, do a girl in.
(T.S. Eliot, 'Sweeney Agonistes')

When female nature, naturally so perverse, becomes sublime
through holiness, then it can be the noblest vehicle of grace.
(Umberto Eco, *The Name of the Rose*)

Women can avoid pollution by a negation of their femaleness, by ridding themselves of the taint of Nature; paradoxically, they can attain ideal femininity by denying what
makes them women—their female bodies—and this is a
denial which in its perfection leads to death. A 'lily' quality of
lifeless purity characterizes the heroine of 'Amy' (1831), a
'virgin blossom . . . never . . . a soul more mild or holier', and
she establishes a model of incorporeality which Tennyson's
future pure woman will follow:

> . . . black hair uncurled and straightly parted
> Upon her marble brow.
> O shape more slender than the fabled fairy . . .
> O long black hair! O pale thin hands!
> ('Amy', 52–7)

Thin and bloodless, Amy is, of course, sexless: 'You love me
not as man [but as a] heavenly spouse.' Amy's bloodlessness
can be contrasted with the pagan earthiness of the woman in
a sonnet of the same date:

She took the dappled partridge fleckt with blood,
    And in her hand the drooping pheasant bare,
    And by his feet she held the woolly hare,
And like a master-painting where she stood,
Lookt some new Goddess of an English wood . . .
    And in one image Life and Death reposed,
    To make my love an Immortality.
(Sonnet, 'She took the dappled partridge', 1–14)

Both women lead to death, but one is the death of bloodless transcendence and the other of life's mortal nature, its violence and shame. Both are aspects of a dualist philosophy of mind and matter, spirit and flesh, in which women can be used to represent either term in these dualities. Their bodies, particularly in the bloody generative processes of menstruation and parturition, remind men too much of their own mortality. Yet because women are, by nature, so polluted, their transcendence of the body's functions is the more exacting and therefore the more significant. A total conquest of her body, her blood, makes of a woman, iconographically, the means by which men attempt to deny the materiality which woman in her other polluted aspect, also represents. Tennyson recognized the equivocal position woman occupies in the dichotomy between flesh and spirit in his placing of the Holy Nun, Percival's mystical sister, at the centre of 'The Holy Grail' (altering his source in Malory to do so) as the instigator of the doomed quest for the Sangrail.

Several of Tennyson's poems portray women who trancend their mortality by the rejection of mortal processes, by the body's attenuation into romanticized tranquillity and permanence, into an image: 'A perfect form in perfect rest' ('The Sleeping Beauty', 24). This is exemplified in the death of the Lady of Shalott, whose 'blood was frozen slowly', and whose 'eyes were darkened wholly': 'A gleaming shape she floated by, / Dead pale between the houses high' (147–57). It is a withdrawal from life, a transformation into a voice, a name, an image of 'a lovely face' which death has saved from the pollution of living.

This choice of pure death over living corruption is developed in 'Lancelot and Elaine', the longer version of

'The Lady of Shalott', published nearly thirty years after
that poem in 1859: '"Him or death," she muttered, "death or
him," / Again and like a burthen, "Him or death"' (897–8).
Elaine's choice of death ensures her purity, 'like a star in
blackest night', and also her permanence. Although her voice
is silenced, and her oarsman dumb, the letter of her life and
love survives; in the same way as the Lady of Shalott
inscribes her name on her boat and on her legend, Elaine's
letter remains to tell her history, and her mysterious and
unsullied death transforms her into an image resisting
change and appropriation:

> ... the dead,
> Oared by the dumb, went upward with the flood—
> In her right hand the lily, in her left
> The letter—all her bright hair streaming down—
> (1146–9)

This poem, like 'The Lady of Shalott', ends at the point of
reduction to an image of purified stasis; other poems, such as
'The Sleeping Beauty' and *The Princess*, record the moment
of the woman's awakening to an apparently successful but
unrecorded future. It is in *Maud* that Tennyson fully
exposes the intractable irresolutions in the notion of woman
as 'twy-natured', as pure essence and as polluted life-giver.

The nameless speaker of *Maud* is violently and hysteric-
ally born into the poem in a re-enactment of a loathed primal
scene of birth and death, of male rivalry and female
suffering, of blood and lust: 'the place and the pit and the
fear' (I.64). *Maud* is a poem about the desire not to have
been born, or since that cannot be, about the desire to undo
the flaw of the speaker's birth, to start again without the taint
of mortality. Like the other son in the poem, Maud's
brother, who carries the sign of his mother in the ring of hair
he wears at the moment of death—like all men, in fact—the
speaker of *Maud* carries the legacy of his mother's sexual
fall ('I heard the shrill-edged shriek of a mother divide
the shuddering night' (I.16)), and this remembered shriek,
the 'blot upon the brain / That *will* show itself without'

(II.200–1), can only be erased by a woman of lifeless purity:
'Luminous, gemlike, ghostlike, deathlike'. Maud's 'cold and
clear-cut face . . . Passionless, pale, cold face, star-sweet on a
gloom profound' (I.88–91) appears to offer escape from the
mortal state the speaker's mother has left him in; as the 'milk
white fawn . . . all unmeet for a wife', she opposes the
maternal principle of birth and blood and death. In the logic
of such thinking, Maud should die at this point, transcend
her mortality as her mother, 'mute in her grave as her image in
marble above', has done. There, of course, is the paradox the
poem struggles with; Maud must die to save herself from—
death. The poem warns of this; within the terms of its self-
hatred, no matter how the nature of woman is questioned,
and her complicity as scapegoat or redeemer courted, the
answer to the problem of living is death: 'And Echo there,
whatever is asked her, answers "Death"' (I.4). It is enough
to make a man mad.

Tennyson's description of *Maud* as 'a little *Hamlet*' and
his choice of a monodramatic form for his poem should alert
us to the parallels and also to the revisions he made in this
deliberate rereading of Shakespeare's play. Each work is, as
Tennyson noted, 'the history of a morbid, poetic soul' to
whom is offered a pure young woman as saviour; for just as
Ophelia is proposed as a solution to Hamlet's 'morbidity', his
sense 'That it were better my mother had not borne me'
(III.i.125), so Maud is proposed as 'the one bright thing to
save / My yet young life in the wilds of Time' (I.556–7). Both
Ophelia and Maud are caught up in an ideology which,
condemning them to both idealization and loathing, leads to
their destruction. But Ophelia's confusion at the double
nature of women—nuns or breeders of sinners—emerges in
Maud as the speaker's dilemma. Although Hamlet claims
that it 'hath made me mad', the weight of the paradox rests on
Ophelia and it is she who really does go mad, just as the
speaker of *Maud* goes mad. Her madness is internalized in
him, rewritten in the anxieties and delusions of mid-
Victorian manhood as they are extremely, but not untruth-
fully, expressed in *Maud*. The requirements of the mono-
drama ensure this solipsism, in which Maud exists only as an

imagined projection of idealized girlhood which the protagonist subjects to change in a tragic and doomed attempt to
infuse life into his 'faultily faultless ... splendidly null'
creation. But this awakening involves her transformation
into another image, the rose image of polluted womanhood,
of the blood of mortality. That this would happen is signalled
in the not quite marmoreal nature of the image the speaker
first conceives of her; although 'perfectly beautiful', there is,
as Tennyson strikingly says, 'an hour's defect of the rose'
(I.84), and it is this defect which will bring the blood to her
veins and, eventually, the hero back to 'the red-ribbed
hollow' of self-loathing. The Pygmalian moment, when the
lily begins ineluctably to redden into the rose, when one
image begins to be transmogrified into its opposite, occurs,
as so often in Victorian writing, with a blush:

> She came to the village church,
> And sat by a pillar alone;
> An angel watching an urn
> Wept over her, carved in stone;
> And once, but once, she lifted her eyes,
> And suddenly, sweetly, strangely blushed
> To find they were met by my own;
>
> (I.301–7)

It is not only the man's gaze, the male act of possession, but
also the woman's consciousness of this act— '... she lifted
her eyes ... To find they were met by my own' ... —which
begins the fall. To remain venerably intact, an image must be
as static as the angel 'carved in stone' (although even this
seems to be dissolving in tears); to be summoned into life by
reciprocating the speaker's desire is to be involved in the
speaker's own fallen state and to implicate them both in
mortality. This moment in *Maud* recalls a similar one in
'The Miller's Daughter' (quoted p. 103)—'And when I
raised my eyes above / They met with two so full and
bright— / Such eyes'—but in this early, happier (and
unique) poem, the image of the woman is less austerely
invested with her purity—'A glowing arm, a gleaming neck'
(78)—and so the transition to the narrative of the senses and
the emotions is possible to achieve.

Beyond this point of awakening in *Maud* there is a brief
and ecstatic moment of transition, epitomizing the very
essence and centre of romantic love when consummation is
anticipated but not yet achieved and the inevitable difference
it creates not yet experienced, when Maud can be both pure
and passionate, 'Queen lily and rose in one' (I.905). But her
'twy-natured' condition pulls in two directions, although
both of them lead to death. Her purity is associated with the
death of withdrawal from life: '[I] knew that the death-white
curtain meant but sleep, / Yet I shuddered and thought like a
fool of the sleep of death' (I.525–6). And as for roses, the
poem will show that 'they are not roses but blood' (II.316).
As the sexual excitement in the poem rises, in particular as
Maud is the more perceived as a desiring as well as a desirable
woman—'Ah, be / Among the roses tonight' (I.848–9) is her
message to the speaker—so the speaker is delivered once
again into that murderous primal scene:

> And there rises ever a passionate cry
> From underneath in the darkening land—
> What is it, that has been done?
> O dawn of Eden bright over earth and sky,
> The fires of Hell brake out of thy rising sun,
> The fires of Hell and of Hate;
>
> (II.5–10)

Maud's later transformation, after this black Genesis, into a
double-natured ghost, a vengeful 'ghastly Wraith' and a
blessed spirit, is a mocking, ghostly repetition of the
speaker's dilemma. In the protagonist's departure for the
Crimean War, *Maud* anticipates 'Enoch Arden': the precipitate bid for action, the suicidal flight into danger, are
evasions of a psychic problem within the individual protagonists, and also within the poems. For although the
'blood-red blossom of war' in some respects is a congruent
conclusion to the rose-sexuality-mortality thread running
throughout *Maud*, there is a residue of emotion, in particular
to do with the 'pure and true' aspects of the love for Maud,
which cannot be accommodated into the Jingoistic militarism
of the conclusion of the poem. Tennyson's inability to

resolve the issues the poem has raised are evident in his
indecisiveness over its ending; the first edition of 1855 ended
at line 53, and in response to criticism of this bellicose and
incongruous note, Tennyson drafted a conclusion in which
the protagonist's new purpose is arrived at 'By the light of a
love not lost, with a purer mind'. But in subsequent drafts,
and in the final six lines as they were published from 1856
onwards, this line was abandoned along with any other
attempt to relate the issues harmoniously (Shatto 1986; p.
157). The platitudinous conclusion as it now stands (54–9)
seems a suggestive evasion, an admission that the ghosts of
Maud, 'spectral bride' or 'dream [of] a dear delight', cannot
be laid to rest but escape the narrative of the poem as an
unresolved problem. *Maud,* surely Tennyson's most pessimistic poem, acknowledges how absurd, absurd to the point
of madness and self-destruction, yet how imperative, given
the fallen state of man's birth, is the attempt to escape his
humanity.

The quest for the pure, unfleshly woman is concluded in
'The Holy Grail' with a tacit recognition of the destructive
extremes to which the sexual logic of *Maud* may be pursued.
Percival's sister, the Holy Nun in 'The Holy Grail', is a
culmination of Tennyson's bloodless and bodiless maidens:

> And so she prayed and fasted, till the sun
> Shone, and the wind blew, through her, and I
>   thought
> She might have risen and floated when I saw her.
>   (98–100)

It is her pure and devotional life which brings the Holy
Grail, the vessel from which Christ drank at the Last
Supper, back to an 'adulterous race' that has lost its spiritual
bearings. The nun's first vision of the Grail in Tennyson's
poem is based on more matter-of-fact sightings of it in
Malory, Tennyson's source, including one by Lancelot:

> And with that he saw the chamber door open, and there came
> out a great clearness, that the house was as bright as all the

torches of the world had been there . . . and [he] saw a table of
silver, and the holy vessel, covered with red samite. (*Le Morte
Darthur,* XVII.15)

In Tennyson this becomes:

> and then
> Streamed through my cell a cold and silver beam,
> And down the long beam stole the Holy Grail,
> Rose-red with beatings in it, as if alive,
> Till all the white walls of my cell were dyed
> With rosy colours leaping on the wall;
> And then the music faded, and the Grail
> Past, and the beam decayed, and from the walls
> The rosy quiverings died into the night.
>   (115–23)

In this lurid transformation Tennyson disconcertingly juxt-
aposes the bloodlessness of 'the pale nun' with the pulsating
Grail which is like a heart or a womb torn from a living body.
The passage is a variant of the rose-and-lily imagery
Tennyson has used before and it tracks an orgasmic rise and
fall similar to the central sections of *Maud*. But the nun's
ecstasy is a religious one and although Tennyson could align
his writing with a tradition of mystical-sexual writing from
the Song of Songs to Hopkins to authorize his practice here,
it is nevertheless disturbing (not least in the startling
alteration of the by no means squeamish Malory) to find the
religious experience of the Grail, the core of the Arthurian
story, expressed in such carnal terms. For it is as though the
nun's human passions, her body (which, we are told, once
'glowed . . . with such a fervent flame of human love' (72–4)),
have become the Grail, the complement and sign of her
purity, outside of her yet invasive, the ultimate of her
spiritual longing. The truth the nun illustrates is that the
more the body is banished, the more powerfully it returns,
revealing how inextricable is its link with the spirit. Arthur
calls the Grail 'A sign to maim this Order which I made'
(297); of course his mistrustful Protestantism, Tennyson's
own, is concerned to show the 'spiritual waste' of the

visionary life for all but a very few. But his words also have
relevance to the position of 'The Holy Grail' in relation to the
rest of the Tennyson canon; published in 1869, one of the
last of the *Idylls* and, indeed, one of Tennyson's last long
poems (he was to be increasingly occupied with the writing
of drama from this time to his death in 1892), 'The Holy
Grail', in the figure of the nun and her vision, admits the
indissolubility of mind and matter, impure body and pure
spirit. Up to this point, certainly up to *Maud*, a kind of
precarious order has prevailed based on the division of the
two, a division which found its most expressive locus, and
also ultimately its undoing, in the divergent images of
women Tennyson has employed.

CHAPTER 10

Women, Desire and Grief

Everywoman is endowed with the general essence of Woman,
and therefore of the Mother. . . . She is all that man desires and
all that he does not attain. She is the good mediatrix between
propitious Nature and man; and she is the temptation of un-
conquered Nature, counter to all goodness. (Simone de Beauvoir,
The Second Sex)

> Whateer I see, whereer I move
> These whispers rise and fall away;
> Something of pain, of loss, of love,
> But what, twere hard to say.
> ('One of the earliest surviving ex-
> amples of [Tennyson's] verse,
> written when he was about eight'
> (Martin 1980; p. 22))

> Softly, in the dusk, a woman is singing to me
> Taking me back down the vista of years . . .
> . . . The glamour
> Of childish days is upon me, my manhood is cast
> Down in the flood of remembrance, I weep like a
> child for the past.
> (D.H. Lawrence, 'Piano')

In the preceding chapters Tennyson has emerged as a
misogynist poet to whom women, if not in life then at least in
the imaginative scheme his poetry offers, represent fear and
loathing and, even more invidious, self-loathing. As the

141

expectation of love dies, so the hatred of women grows until in some of his poems, 'Lucretius', for example, the misogyny is so virulent and indiscriminate as to become self-cancelling in that one is amazed and impressed (though no less distressed) at the power women apparently possess. Such a response prompts one to ask why this power exists in men's imaginings, particularly since there seems to be so little evidence of it in the 'real' world of social and economic relations. Perhaps the answer lies in the life of the individual man, not meaning Tennyson's own life, his biography, but the process of becoming an adult that each individual man goes through and that Tennyson's poetry demonstrates. In this respect his poetic development, from the early search in romantic love for a unified Self to his maturity amongst the perilously fracturing constructs of masculinity and femininity his culture offered him, can be read as an exemplary paradigm of what constitutes maleness, not only in the Victorian age but in Western patriarchal thought in general, in which the perception of women is that they betray the nobility men entrust to them.

To explain this perception as one of differentiation, as Virginia Woolf's 'looking-glass' theory does, is right as far as it goes, but as an explanation it doesn't go far enough to account for the complex mixture of contempt and idealization with which men regard women. For it seems that in the disproportion and inappropriateness of men's imaginings about women, in what men say about women, in the story men tell (whether it is in the *Sun* newspaper or *Anna Karenina* or Tennyson's 'Lucretius') of the loss of love, the impossibility of desire, the growth of fear and bitterness, there is more of grief and anger than the current situation justifies, as if ancient disappointments were being relived through present discontents, old disillusionments confirmed, old scores settled, a 'dark undercurrent of woe', as the speaker in *Maud* expresses it, which can never be assuaged. If this is so, then men's grievance belongs to the past: it is a grief pertaining to what has happened long ago, what has been formative in the growth of a self which can scarcely forgive the processes and agents of its own attainment.

In Memoriam is a narrative of grievance as well as a narrative of grief; it blames women for its sorrow in the sense that they represent what can never be attained: they are the impossible desire, the non-death of the already dead friend. In loss we look to what is different from ourselves to give shape and body to our bereavement; because it is different, it stands for what we do not possess, for what is not ourselves. In men's relationship to what is most different from themselves, women, lies the substance of all male loss, of all that separates them from wholeness, from what they desire and are irrevocably denied. Loss is located within sexual difference.

Writing is also a kind of loss; what was once part of the writer is now separate, different, spent. Perhaps this is doubly true of elegy; the poet's grief is lost to him twice over, by being cast in words in the first place, and also by its distance from him as the object, no longer the subject, of his grief and complaint. As Tennyson says, it is 'half a sin / To put in words the grief I feel' (*In Memoriam* V.1–2). Being so distant, so separate, writing becomes the Other of the writing Self, in the case of a male poet, the female Other of the male poetic Self. Tennyson expresses this idea in traditional terms in his reference to his muse, 'My Melpomene', who describes herself as '"an earthly Muse . . . owning but a little art / To lull with song an aching heart, / And render human love his dues"' (XXXVII.9–16). Elegy is therefore doubly female, in a manner of speaking, in that femaleness is its buried theme—woman as the irrevocably lost—and it is also the act of writing, the unstable female Otherness of male creativity. In this double relationship to the female, elegy conspicuously exposes an instability and insecurity within the writing process. Even in Tennyson's own terms there are dangerous discordances, for although his Muse may appear obedient and humble, the very fact of her being female, the constructs of femininity on which she is built, introduce wayward elements into the relationship; she has 'a touch of shame upon her cheek' (10) and, as she describes it, she '"loitered in the master's field"' (23) and her utterance, the very act of her speaking, is a kind of profanity: '"And

darkened sanctities with song"' (24). The complex resonances
of *In Memoriam* derive from this kind of playful but also
painfully difficult discovery of incompatability and loss
within the scene of sexual difference, a scenario which
constitutes a buried 'autobiography' in the poem. For if the
poem is ostensibly a poem about the death of a friend, it is
subterraneously a poem about many other anxieties which
crowd in upon the 'empty space' (Eagleton 1978; p. 104)
which the friend's death makes available in poetic discourse.
And chiefly, Hallam's death provokes a crisis of self-
formation, a compulsive retelling of the story of what makes
a man, particularly what makes a man in relation to women.

*   *   *

Tennyson's telling of this personal history of maleness
occupied seventeen years of his life, from the time immediately after his hearing of Arthur Hallam's death in October
1833 to the publication of the completed sequence in June
1850. His moulding of this body of grief comprised a slow
and indecisive accretion of parts eventually totalling 129
sections (two sections, XXXIX and LIX, were added in
1869 and 1851 respectively), plus an Introduction and an
Epilogue. In general outline, this long, painfully-written
poem constitutes a narrative of mourning: that is, it struggles
to register the shock of Arthur's death, is incredulous that it
has happened yet is forced to accept that it has, frequently
recalls the dead man, commits him to memory and com-
memorates him, is finally resigned to what has happened and
looks forward to new life and love in the future whilst not
forgetting the past. In these respects, the progress of *In
Memoriam* follows that of 'normal' mourning; it conforms to
'the work which mourning performs':

> Reality-testing [shows] that the loved object no longer exists,
> and it proceeds to demand that all libido shall be withdrawn
> from its attachments to that object. . . . Nevertheless its orders
> cannot be obeyed at once. They are carried out bit by bit, at
> great expense of time and cathectic energy, and in the meantime
> the existence of the lost object is psychically prolonged. Each

single one of the memories and expectations in which the libido
is bound to the object is brought up and hyper-cathected, and
detachment of the libido is accomplished in respect of it ...
when the work of mourning is completed the ego becomes free
and uninhibited again. (Freud 1957; pp. 244–5)

Adequate as this description is as a synopis of what happens
in *In Memoriam*, it does, however, overlook several elements
both concerning the poem and also intrinsic to it. In the first
place, there is the poem's exceptionally long gestation; there
have been few works where there has been such a to-do about
the writing of it, such delay between the occasion of the poem
(the friend's death) and the public celebration of that
occasion (the poem's publication). There is something
gratuitous about the process, something excessive. There is
also a quality of excess in the poem's length, the obsessive
accumulation of its parts, the unrelenting march of its
proceeding, the repetitive monotony of its rhyme scheme
and its stunted lines. Sensing the poem's tense self-discipline
and its straining rationality, Fitzgerald not inappropriately
described it as having 'the air of being evolved by a Poetical
Machine of the highest order' (quoted Martin 1980; p. 330).

There is also *within* the poem a sense of something extra,
gratuitous, to the business of mourning. Of course, Tennyson
is writing in an elegiac tradition, which includes *Lycidas* and
Adonais, in which extravagant and excessive displays of
emotion are a requirement of the form, and *In Memoriam*
partakes of the structures and rhetoric of this convention of
excess. But *In Memoriam* goes beyond the conventional,
particularly in a tendency for grief to be displaced into
disproportionate self-abasement, into terror (sometimes of a
suicidal kind) and nihilism. For example, the mourner is
'like a guilty thing' (VII.7), he is not 'worthy even to speak' of
the dead man (XXXVII.11) and he wonders 'How should
[the dead man] love a thing so low?' (LX.16). At some
stages, the mourner's desire is 'to sink to peace. ... To drop
head-foremost in the jaws / Of vacant darkness and to cease
(XXXIV.13–16), and at others 'the blood creeps, and the
nerves prick / And tingle; and the heart is sick, / And all the

wheels of Being slow' (L.2–4). In addition, there is running
throughout the poem a curious kind of physical disgust, in
particular a displacement of grief into imagery of terrifying
birth or sexual activity:

>   ... yawning doors,
> And shoals of pucker'd faces drive;
> Dark bulks that tumble half alive,
> And lazy lengths on boundless shores;
>   (LXX.9–12)

Even in a domestic section such as VI, where there is an
analogy established between the poet's loss and that of a
father, a mother and a sweetheart, the surface is disturbed by
dark connotations:

> O father, whereso'er thou be,
>   Who pledgest now thy gallant son;
>   A shot, ere half thy draught be done,
> Hath stilled the life that beat from thee.
>
> O mother, praying God will save
>   Thy sailor,—while thy head is bowed,
>   His heavy-shotted hammock-shroud
> Drops in his vast and wandering grave. ...
>
> O somewhere, meek, unconscious dove,
>   That sittest ranging golden hair;
>   And glad to find thyself so fair,
> Poor child, that waitest for thy love!
>
> For now her father's chimney glows
>   In expectation of a guest;
>   And thinking 'this will please him best,'
> She takes a riband or a rose;
>
> For he will see them on tonight;
>   And with the thought her colour burns;
>   And, having left the glass, she turns
> Once more to set a ringlet right;

> And, even when she turned, the curse
> Had fallen, and her future Lord
> Was drowned in passing through the ford,
> Or killed in falling from his horse.
>   (VI.9–40)

Here the act of fathering a child ('the life that beat from thee') seems inextricably associated with the son's death: 'a shot . . . Hath stilled the life.' Similarly, the crouching mother, who as it were gives birth to, 'drops', her son into his grave and makes of his caul his shroud, links birth to death. And, in a parody of the action of 'The Lady of Shalott', the girl who turns back in narcissistic desire to her mirror becomes her lover's killer: 'even when she turned, the curse / Had fallen.'

For such profound unease and revulsion, which seems disproportionate to, even though occasioned by, the death of a friend, Freud has a different name, 'melancholia'. As a condition, this has a good deal in common with mourning: a 'profoundly painful dejection, cessation of interest in the outside world, loss of the capacity to love [and] an inhibition of all activity'. Additionally, however, there is a 'lowering of self-regarding feelings to a degree that finds utterance in self-reproaches and self-revilings, and culminates in a delusional expectation of punishment' (Freud 1957; p. 244). Melancholia does not necessarily, or usually, have an object to its sense of loss, or it may be that there is not a direct correlation between the lost object and the sense of loss ('a loss has occurred but one cannot see clearly what it is that has been lost') or that the patient is aware of the loss 'but only in the sense that he knows *whom* he has lost but not *what* he has lost in him'. 'This would suggest', Freud continues, 'that melancholia is in some way related to an object-loss which is withdrawn from consciousness, in contradistinction to mourning, in which there is nothing about the loss that is unconscious' (Freud 1957; p. 245). The essence of Freud's argument is that mourning is the suffering of a loss in regard to an object; melancholia is a loss in regard to one's ego. Although Freud does not say so, there is obviously a conflict inherent in the relationship between mourning and melancholia. One is a process, essentially a healing one, which seeks to restore the ego to an uninhibited state; the other, melancholia, is a sickness, a condition restraining the ego within a state of depressive narcissism.

In a moving essay, 'Mourning and its Relation to Manic Depressive States', written in 1938 not long after the death of her son from a climbing accident, Melanie Klein sought to extend Freud's ideas by relating adult mourning to certain stages in infant development which if successfully gone through stabilize the child's ego, or, in the case of an adult, bring the griever back to life. If not successfully accomplished, manic-depressive states in the infant and abnormal mourning (that is, melancholia) in the adult are the result.

The basis of Klein's thought in this respect is the infant's relationship to the first love-object of its life, the breast, which is both a good and a bad object: good in that it supplies security and nourishment, bad in that it also represents loss and denial of all that is good. In normal development, the baby's internalization of the good breast—that is, its belief that the good breast will not forsake it forever, that it will return, and that in its absence the image of the good breast will balance the sorrow and loss caused by that absence (the bad breast)—is a major element in ego stability. In a sense, the individual carries the good breast, the good mother (or parents), around as an image for the rest of life, and this enables the individual to make a 'correct' correlation between the internal imagos and the occurrences, people and things of the outside world. If this correlation and proportioning mechanism breaks down or is not established, then paranoia, psychosis, melancholia, or anxiety develop to varying degrees. Klein maintains that 'a satisfactory relation to people and to reality depends upon the child's success in his struggles against the chaos inside him and [upon his] having securely established his "good" internal objects'. The learning process involved here, which is a coming to terms with loss and the bad feelings this gives rise to, is a kind of mourning, an infantile neurosis taking the forms of pining and mania. Klein's particular insight is to suggest that adult mourning reactivates this early learning process with all its painfulness and uncertainties; in other words, adult bereavement re-enacts infantile depression, and, at the same time, threatens the security of the internalized 'good objects'. Freud had maintained that in mourning, the individual absorbs the lost love objects within his own ego; Klein's point is that

> he is not doing it for the first time but, through the work of mourning, is reinstating that object as well as all his loved *internal* objects which he feels he has lost. He is therefore *recovering* what he had already attained in childhood. . . . In normal mourning the individual re-introjects and reinstates, as well as the actual lost person, his loved parents—who are felt to be his 'good' inner objects. His inner world, the one which he has built up from his earliest days onwards, in his fantasy was destroyed when the actual loss occurred. The rebuilding of this inner world characterizes the successful work of mourning. (Klein 1986; pp. 166–7)

Klein points out what *In Memoriam* demonstrates, that 'Many mourners can only make slow steps in re-establishing the bonds with the external world because they are struggling against the chaos inside'. In these terms *In Memoriam* can be seen as a poem of mourning which is fathomed by melancholia: that is, it seeks to instate within the ego of the mourner the lost love object of Hallam—to remember with love but without undue grief—but it does so in the face of an internal chaos which is re-enacting an unresolved loss, a pining and mania, as Klein expresses it, deriving from a primal loss. The desire for the lost friend is rivalled and invaded by desire of another kind, by other emotions—fugitive, contingent, of uncertain and inexplicable relevance. The acknowledged narrative of bereavement is accompanied by another narrative of loss which derives from long ago, from a hidden but ever present past. It is the 'autobiography' of a lost self which is being written at the same time as an elegy for a friend.

This was recognized as long ago as 1946 by W.H. Auden:

> In no other English poet of comparable rank does the bulk of his work seem so clearly to be inspired by some single and

probably very early experience. Tennyson's own description of himself as

> An infant crying in the night;
> An infant crying for the light:

> And with no language but a cry

is extraordinarily acute. If Wordsworth is the great English poet of Nature, then Tennyson is the great English poet of the Nursery. (Auden 1946; p. xv)

Tennyson seems to have recognized it himself: in the summary description he gives of *In Memoriam* in both the Introduction and the Epilogue, when he looks back on the process of writing (the Introduction was written in 1849, just before publication), it appears to him as a distant utterance, something from long ago, something, in fact, that belongs to childhood: 'echoes out of weaker times' (Epil. 22), 'wild and wandering cries, / Confusions of a wasted youth' (Introd. 41–2). But although he can thus disarmingly dismiss his work's 'weakness', its very strength and its enduring appeal lies in the fraught relationship it establishes between the present and the buried past, between the adult grief and the infant crying in the night, between the dead friend and the other troubled figures of loss that haunt the poem. Hallam's death raises questions about the stability and permanence of the self (what purpose does an individual life serve? what is its nature after death? and so on) which the poem seeks to answer at the level of rational debate but it also connects these anxieties of the adult philosophizing mind with the anxieties of an infant self reliving early experiences of separation and individuation.

Appropriately enough, Hallam himself had written about the child's growth into individuality in his essay 'On Sympathy', which describes the process by which the individual perceives itself as distinct from other human beings and the material world. In the earliest pre-conscious state of being, Hallam argues, the 'soul [has] attributed itself to every consciousness' and to all objects, so that, for example, 'the infant cannot separate the sensations of nourishment from the form of his nurse or mother' (Motter 1943; pp. 133–4). Hallam's argument is conducted to show that the human ability to sympathize stems from this erstwhile identification with other states of being. Tennyson's translation of these ideas into his own terms occurs in section XLV of *In Memoriam*:

> The baby new to earth and sky,
>   What time his tender palm is prest
>   Against the circle of the breast,
> Has never thought that 'this is I:'
>
> But as he grows he gathers much,
>   And learns the use of 'I', and 'me',
>   And finds 'I am not what I see,
> And other than the things I touch.'
>
> So rounds he to a separate mind
>   From whence clear memory may begin,
>   As through the frame that binds him in
> His isolation grows defined.
>
> This use may lie in blood and breath,
>   Which else were fruitless of their due,
>   Had man to learn himself anew
> Beyond the second birth of Death.

In the thinking of Hallam and Tennyson, and in Klein's formulation of the theory too, the nurse or the mother, the breast, becomes associated with the state of non-individuation before 'isolation grows defined'. The growing process involved in self-definition, the 'gathering' and 'rounding', to use Tennyson's terms, is painful as well as socially essential, and feelings of hurt and anger at what the child is losing become attached to the female figure associated with growth, as well as those feelings of desire and longing for what is being lost. And by extension all females, in this imaginative scheme, become associated with loss and desire, and with the anger and longing that their presence and absence have aroused. Certainly, this seems to be what is happening in *In Memoriam*; Hallam's death re-activates, as Klein suggests it

can do, the pining and mania which belong to the child's
early breast relation and these emotions are reconstituted as
the narrative of melancholia in the adult poem. *In Memoriam*'s
many female presences carry this 'other' narrative of fear and
longing which exists in addition to and struggling against the
narrative of mourning. As Barthes suggests in 'The Absent
One', there is a constant rehearsal of infant longing in adult
longing, and a re-enactment of the struggle to forget the
absence of the loved one:

> I diligently obey the training by which I was very early
> accustomed to be separated from my mother—which nonethe-
> less remained, at its source, a matter of suffering (not to
> say hysteria). I behave as a well-weaned subject; I can feed
> myself, *meanwhile*, on other things besides the maternal
> breast.
>   This endured absence is nothing more nor less than forgetful-
> ness. I am, intermittently, unfaithful. This is the condition of
> my survival; for if I did not forget, I should die. The lover who
> doesn't forget *sometimes* dies of excess, exhaustion, and tension
> of memory. (Barthes 1979; p. 14)

The struggle to behave like a 'well-weaned subject', to forget so
as not to die, is apparent in a group of sections, a sub-narrative
within *In Memoriam*, in which Sorrow is consistently
personified as a woman: III, XVI, XXXIX, XLVIII, LIX.
In the metaphor involved in this personification, the vehicle of
the metaphor—the female forms Sorrow takes—overpowers
its tenor—the abstraction Sorrow; this is an overpowering
which disturbs by its disproportion and loss of decorum. Yet
at the same time, it is all too appropriate that Sorrow, as the
emotion of loss and desire, should be characterized as
female. The terms of such characterization are inevitably
those of (Victorian) sexual stereotypes: the whore, the
flirtatious maiden, the mistress and the wife, almost the same
examples Tennyson provided in the first four parts of *Idylls
of the King* published in 1859. When Sorrow is most
importunate and debilitating, she appears as a loathed yet
fascinating spectre from the Victorian underworld, the
necrophiliac, disease-ridden whore:

O Priestess in the vaults of Death,
O sweet and bitter in a breath,
What whispers from thy lying lip? . . .

And shall I take a thing so blind,
  Embrace her as my natural good;
  Or crush her, like a vice of blood,
Upon the threshold of the mind?
                    (III.2–4, 13–16)

This punitive and destructive figure is slightly moderated in
section XVI but here she still appears as capricious and
wanton, a succubus who has taken away 'my power to think /
And all my knowledge of myself; / And made me that
delirious man' (15–17). In section XLVIII (and to some
extent in sections XXI and XXIII also), it is Sorrow's
expressive and intuitive powers which are dwelt on. Her
female attributes are not those of reason: her care is not,
'to part and prove' (XLVIII.5), but with a becoming super-
ficiality 'to sport . . . with words [and] loosen . . . from the lip
/ Short swallow-flights of song, that dip / Their wings in
tears, and skim away' (11–16). The climax of this sequence
occurs in section LIX in which Sorrow is offered a choice—
'O Sorrow wilt thou live with me / No casual mistress, but a
wife' (1–2)—in which new relationship Sorrow will 'rule [the
speaker's] blood' as a 'centred passion' and her caprice be
contained within legitimized sexual activity: 'But I'll have
leave at times to play / As with the creature of my love' (11–
12). In this scheme, Sorrow's disreputable past, under the
mourner's newly acquired patronage and mastery of her, will
be almost forgotten:

And set thee forth, for thou art mine,
  With so much hope for years to come,
  That, howsoe'er I know thee, some
Could hardly tell what name were thine.
                    (LIX.13–16)

In the movement through these sections, which is also a
movement through manic manifestations of loss, the mourner

has eventually exerted some control over the wayward but as yet unforgiven female energies that threaten him. Sorrow must be contained and 'her' excesses brought into civilized relationship (marriage) with her possessor. But this has not yet accomplished the work of mourning; the griever's relationship with his loss is still a suspicious one and she is captive within his possession, not freely loving. To purge the melancholia, to complete the mourning, the griever must experience his loss in many ways and many times, only gradually and by no means consistently working through his anger and sorrow. As Klein says:

> Through tears . . . the mourner not only expresses feeling and this eases tension, but also expels his 'bad' feelings and 'bad' objects. . . . At this stage in mourning, suffering can be productive [although] inner security comes about not by a straightforward movement but in waves. (Klein 1986; pp. 162–4)

The point in *In Memoriam* at which the group concerning Sorrow is concluded is not yet a stage at which the mourner is secure in the re-establishment of his internal good objects; as we have seen, the attitude towards Sorrow is hostile and recriminatory, and the trope pertaining to it is exhausted in its forward movement and still remains tinged with melancholia, one of the many abortive attempts to carry mourning to its conclusion. But in the more sustained use of nature imagery, particularly in its relation to places familiar to the griever and his friend, the female presences eventually become restorative and forgiving, entering the poem as mothering figures who liberate the child-mourner into new life. Although *In Memoriam* does engage in the debate on Nature which will be carried to such hostile excesses in 'Lucretius', in its progressive and eventually forgiving search for the Mother, it is able to liberate Nature into benevolence and into agreement with Klein when she says: '"Nature mourns with the mourner", I believe that Nature in this connection represents the internal good mother' (Klein 1986; p. 162).

For example, the late group XCIX–CV, which as a whole

group represents a progression from an earlier sense of
Nature's malignity ('red in tooth and claw' (LVI.15) and
'marked as with some hideous crime' (LXXII.18)), develops
within its sections a process of healing which is more nearly
brought to completion. This begins in XCV with the
momentary communion with Hallam in which the dead
friend is introjected, although only fleetingly, into the
mourner's self:

> The dead man touched me from the past,
> And all at once it seemed at last
> The living soul was flashed on mine ...
>
> (34–6)

This is prepared for, as Ann Wordsworth has shown
(Wordsworth 1981; p. 219) by the representation of Nature
as a solicitous mother:

> ... now we sang old songs that pealed
> From knoll to knoll, where, couched at ease,
> The white kine glimmered, and the trees
> Laid their dark arms about the field.
>
> (13–16)

Although the vision fades—'stricken through with doubt'—
the memory of Hallam as a loving friend is successfully
united with revived internal images of goodness, the mania
and depression are calmed, and reality-testing, which confirms that Hallam is indeed lost, nevertheless recognizes that
not all is lost, that goodness and hope and the lovability of the
griever still exist: 'once more . . . the trees laid their dark arms
about the field: / And sucked from out the distant gloom / A
breeze . . .' (50–2; my italics). The section ends with the
promise that life will 'broaden into boundless day', but although this is a hopeful conclusion, there are still disturbing
elements present in this final scene; the breeze, summoned
to bring fresh life to the dawn, finds vestiges of a melancholic
past in the roses and lilies (always symptomatic of dangerous
sexual polarities in Tennyson); the rose is 'heavy-folded' and
the lilies are 'flung . . . to and fro' and these stifling and

distressed associations render the end of the section uneasy
and unresolved.

A similarly tentative movement is made in section XCIX
which rewrites the terms of communal mourning introduced
in section VI. Nature is now fecund:

> Risest thou thus, dim dawn, again,
>   So loud with voices of the birds,
>   So thick with lowings of the herds,
> Day, when I lost the flower of men;
>   (1–4)

but it is still troubled and tumultuous: 'Day ... Who
tremblest through thy darkling red / On yon swollen brook
that bubbles fast' (4–6). And the allusion to *Othello* in line
13—'Who wakenest with thy balmy breath'—, recalling
Othello's words to Desdemona as he is about to kill her—'Ah
balmy breath, that dost almost persuade / Justice to break her
sword' (V.ii.16–17)—has painful sexual connotations. But
whereas Desdemona wakens only to death, to an act of
supreme persecution by someone who has lost all sense of
internal good, here the day, in its retrospective autumnal
aspect, wakens the world with its balmy breath to a more
balanced apprehension of existence:

> Who wakenest with thy balmy breath
>   To myriads on the genial earth,
>   Memories of bridal, or of birth,
> And unto myriads more, of death.
>
> O wheresoever those may be,
>   Betwixt the slumber of the poles,
>   To-day they count as kindred souls;
> They know me not, but mourn with me.
>   (13–20)

Although Halam is still mourned, and his death, any death,
cannot be denied, yet this does not destroy, is it had done in
earlier times, the mourner's sense of love and community.
This section prepares for his exit from his childhood home in

sections C—CII, a world of infancy which has been re-
entered through the act of mourning, obsessively and angrily
occupied in the melancholia of the earlier part of the poem,
and now gracefully left behind. The process of reinstatement
of early loves, and the growth beyond them, is beautifully
suggested in the listed negatives of section CI:

> Unwatched, the garden bough shall sway ...
> Unloved, that beech will gather brown ...
>
> Unloved, the sun-flower, shining fair,
> Ray round with flames her disk of seed ...
>
> Unloved, by many a sandy bar,
> The brook shall babble down the plain ...
>
> Uncared for, gird the windy grove ...

The section ends with a leave-taking which benignly accepts
separation from the home of childhood and bequeaths that
home to the 'fresh association' which 'the stranger's child'
will bring. As Klein says, 'hatred has receded and love is
freed.' The final lines—'And year by year our memory fades /
From all the *circle* of the hills'—recall section XLV:

> The baby new to earth and *sky*,
>   What time his tender palm is prest
>   Against the *circle* of the breast,
> Has never thought that 'this is I:'
>
> But as he grow[s] ...
> So rounds he to a separate mind ...

But the recollection in CI of this infant loss and separation is
untroubled and leads serenely to the linking of the dead
friend and 'the well-beloved place / Where first we gazed
upon the *sky*' (CII.1–2; my italics). The work of mourning is
nearing completion; not only is the 'separate claim' of both
the 'lost friend' and the 'matin song' of boyhood acknowledged but they are also seen as inextricably connected:

[In] the individual's setting up the lost loved object inside
himself, he is not doing so for the first time but, through the
work of mourning, is reinstating that object as well as all his
loved *internal* objects which he feels he has lost. He is therefore
recovering what he had already attained in childhood. (Klein
1986; pp. 165–6)

> ... but ere we go from home,
> As down the garden-walks I move,
> Two spirits of a diverse love
> Contend for loving masterdom....
>
> I turn to go: my feet are set
> To leave the pleasant fields and farms;
> They mix in one another's arms
> To one pure image of regret.
>   (CII.5–24)

*   *   *

This account of *In Memoriam* makes it appear Tennyson's
most optimistic and balanced poem, the one in which women
are 'forgiven' and the good mother prevails over the bad. In
some respects, such an account echoes previous readings of
In Memoriam (most notably A.C. Bradley's) which have
similarly seen the poem's narrative as a movement from
negative to positive: from despair to hope, from doubt to
faith, and so on. But just as these earlier readings have been
uneasy at their schematizing of a poem the language of which
qualifies all perceived certainties, so a Kleinian reading has
to acknowledge a deconstructive practice within its programme. For if the poem works through melancholia and
mourning to a state of ego equilibrium, *the very process by
which this stability is acquired*—the search for the mother—
baffles and frustrates the progress the poem struggles to
make. The problem has to do with a self-cancelling function
implicit in the writing of elegy.

In the emotional economy of the poem, the female figures,
which have facilitated the act of mourning, have also become
the melancholic location of a superfluity of loss which
Hallam's death instigates and excuses but cannot adequately

account for. Although the poem's resonances depend on this sense of superfluity to its actual occasion, there is a danger to the process of writing poetry inherent in this courting of the world of the unconscious past. This danger relates to the nature of language itself and to the notion of sexual difference which inhabits it. If the mother, and by extension all women, are associated with the undifferentiated Self of infancy which must be painfully lost in order for a separate social Self to be born, then she becomes identified not only with loss but also with a forgotten stage of life prior to the acquisition of language. By contrast, the father, who represents the third term in Freud's 'family romance' and who disturbs the dyad of mother–child, becomes identified with prohibition, individuation, time, order and, most importantly, the world of language. Tennyson seems to have recognized the role of language in the process of the individuation of the Self both in what he says in section XLV and in his use of direct speech: '[He] learns the use of "I," and "me," / And finds "I am not what I see . . .".' In this scheme, the mother, the female, who belongs to the pre-linguistic, unified state of infancy, is associated not only with desire (the longing for what has been lost, and therefore with the elegiac impulse) but with absence, silence, that which pre-dates, underpins and is compensated for by language: in other words, the unconscious. It is in opposition to this that language, which is irredeemably male, takes its being. If, therefore, woman is the 'Other' of signification, then in representational terms she 'signifies' what cannot be spoken of: 'Nothing can be said of the woman', Lacan says. 'By her being in the sexual relation radically Other, in relation to what can be said of the unconscious, the woman is that which relates to this Other' (Lacan 1982; p. 151).

As we have seen, in *In Memoriam* Tennyson displaces his grief into female figures and images, either as the emotional conduits in his relationship with the dead man (see above pp. 78–87) or as the location of what Hallam is only a part of, a re-enactment of: *all* loss, *all* desire. The poem therefore articulates a fantasy of sexual difference in which woman is both the myth of loss and its symptom. That is, as myth she represents all that has been lost, is sought for and desired, including the dead Hallam; in opposition to her, 'the soul of man', as Lacan calls it, takes its being: 'For the soul to come into being, she, the woman, is differentiated from it, and this has always been the case. Called woman (*dit-femme*) and defamed (*diffâme*)' (Lacan 1982; p. 156).

At the same time, the poetic self who speaks about loss does so by permission of and surrender to this Other whose disavowal is a condition of signification. In this sense, woman is the symptom of the male speaker's (poet's) lack, which is a doubling-up of her role as the image of loss; she is, therefore, both stand-in for and cause of the loss.

What makes *In Memoriam* so compelling and erotic a poem is its admission of the desirous nature of loss as 'an infant crying in the night'. But the dangers, as well as the excitements, of this admission are very great. 'I oscillate, I vacillate', says Roland Barthes, 'between the phallic image of the raised arms [of Desire] and the babyish image of the wide-open arms [of Need]' (Barthes 1979; pp. 16–17) and this oscillation is a movement the text of *In Memoriam* describes. When Desire collapses into babyish Need the threat is that of an imminent descent into inarticulateness and silence: the site of the feminine, the symptom and cause of loss, the unconscious—Freud's 'dark continent'—which stands in unspeakable opposition to language. When Tennyson approaches this centre of desire, he risks his anchorage in the symbolic order, the order of language, to do so; he imperils his poet's function because the power of speaking is in danger of engulfment—by the scream, the silence, the O-gape of desire. Within sexual difference, language plays out its own drama, shifting from being towards non-being, from assertion of control and prohibition to the awareness of extinction as it approaches its oppositional sources. Such a drama is enacted with astonishing nakedness in sections III—V:

III

O Sorrow, cruel fellowship,
　O Priestess in the vaults of Death,
　O sweet and bitter in a breath,
What whispers from thy lying lip?

'The stars,' she whispers, 'blindly run;
  A web is woven across the sky;
  From out waste places comes a cry,
And murmurs from the dying sun:

'And all the phantom, Nature, stands—
  With all the music in her tone,
  A hollow echo of my own,—
A hollow form with empty hands.'

And shall I take a thing so blind,
  Embrace her as my natural good;
  Or crush her, like a vice of blood,
Upon the threshold of the mind?

IV

To Sleep I give my powers away;
  My will is bondsman to the dark;
  I sit within a helmless bark,
And with my heart I muse and say:

O heart, how fares it with thee now,
  That thou should'st fail from thy desire,
  Who scarcely darest to inquire,
'What is it makes me beat so low?'

Something it is which thou hast lost,
  Some pleasure from thine early years.
  Break, thou deep vase of chilling tears,
That grief hath shaken into frost!

Such clouds of nameless trouble cross
  All night below the darkened eyes;
  With morning wakes the will, and cries,
'Thou shalt not be the fool of loss.'

V

I sometimes hold it half a sin
  To put in words the grief I feel;
  For words, like Nature, half reveal
And half conceal the Soul within.

But, for the unquiet heart and brain,
   A use in measured language lies;
   The sad mechanic exercise,
Like dull narcotics, numbing pain.

In words, like weeds, I'll wrap me o'er,
   Like coarsest clothes against the cold:
   But that large grief which these enfold
Is given in outline and no more.

The three female figures invoked here—Sorrow, Nature and
Sleep—who compositely suggest the feared presences of
Priestess, Prostitute and Succubus, beckon the conscious
will towards extinction, towards what the sections acknowledge as the 'nameless trouble', the 'Something . . . which
thou hast lost, / Some pleasure from thine early years',
towards the loss not just of Hallam but of all that has been
lost and desired but never possessed because it lies beyond
conscious attainment. But the poem (and indeed any writing
that struggles to 'complete' itself), although aware of an
always threatening collapse and regression into the unconscious past, retains control: language, utterance—and in the
context of its own time *meaningful* utterance—must prevail
otherwise the poem would lapse into silence, or, at best, into
incoherence.

In the sections quoted here the poem contains its anxiety
and recovers its intention to speak its loss either by the use of
metaphor ('like a vice of blood', 'thou deep vase of chilling
tears') which translates and displaces the emotion into
parallels under the control of the conscious mind, or by
openly stating the dilemma it faces: 'With morning wakes the
will, and cries, / "Thou shalt not be the fool of loss".' The
Nature-language debate of section V likewise 'rationalizes'
the issue and concludes appropriately with a metaphor which
invokes in the image of the widow—'In words, like weeds,
I'll wrap me o'er'—the mourning female figure who represents the problematics of the poet's relationship with language
as those of disguise, half-truth and inadequacy.

There is a similar movement in the group of sections,
XXXI—XXXIV, which describe Mary's witnessing of the

raising of Lazarus. This unspeakable experience, which neither Lazarus nor the gospel writer can describe—'He told it not; or something sealed / The lips of that Evangelist'— also silences and subdues Mary:

> Her eyes are homes of silent prayer . . .
>
> Borne down by gladness so complete,
> She bows, she bathes the Saviour's feet
> With costly spikenard and with tears.
> (XXXII.1–12)

In religious terms, Mary represents an unrepresentably mystical experience beyond logic or casuistry; but in the sexual drama of language she is also a stand-in for desire, a 'gladness so complete' for which gesture and attitude—'she bows, she bathes . . . with tears'—, as in a dream, are the only signs. Tennyson's delight at approaching both the 'truth' of revelation and the 'truth' of signification is instantly baffled by the inexpressibility of both. Not only did Lazarus leave 'no record of reply . . . telling what it is to die' (XXXI.6–7) but the introduction of Mary's presence into the poem is the cause of acute representational anxiety. In section XXXIV, not strictly of the Lazarus group but emotionally linked to it, the sense of 'darkness at the core' is equated with uncontrolled poetry, with language at its most fantastic and least ordered, and this leads directly into the image of annihilation, of descent into an unconscious state:

> My own dim life should teach me this,
>   That life shall live for evermore,
>   Else earth is darkness at the core,
> And dust and ashes all that is;
>
> This round of green, this orb of flame,
>   Fantastic beauty; such as lurks
>   In some wild Poet, when he works
> Without a conscience or an aim.
>
> What then were God to such as I?
>   'Twere hardly worth my while to choose

Of things all mortal, or to use
A little patience ere I die;

'Twere best at once to sink to peace,
  Like birds the charming serpent draws,
  To drop head-foremost in the jaws
Of vacant darkness and to cease.

Recovery from the violence and disproportion of this
section, in which the poetry itself seems to be disappearing
into a nadir of incoherence, is made in the following section
(XXXV) where conscious argument is apparently resumed—
'Yet if some voice that man could trust'—, but it is a
precarious hold, and in the final lines of this section the
poetry collapses once again into discordant and disgusted
sexuality far in excess of and invading its rational cause:

O me, what profits it to put
  An idle case? If Death were seen
  At first as Death, Love had not been,
Or been in narrowest working shut,

Mere fellowship of sluggish moods,
  Or in his coarsest Satyr-shape
  Had bruised the herb and crushed the grape,
And basked and battened in the woods.
                                    (17–24)

What is shown as at issue here are not merely sexual ethics or
the impact of evolutionary science but the related and more
fundamental question of what constitutes the subjectivity of
the male poetic self who 'speaks' these lines and whose
authority and autonomy in the act of speaking is constantly
under threat from an invasive sexuality. It is the sexuality not
merely of woman as flesh who distracts man from his
transcendent aspirations but also the sexuality of loss and its
relation to language. 'Language is born of absence', as
Barthes says, and absence is woman. To speak of absence, as
both the elegist and the lover must do, is to summon
woman's presence into the poem and this is to invoke, in an

imprisoning circularity, all that she stands for: silence, undifferentiation, non-being.

In a memorable description, Carlyle said that Tennyson's voice was 'musical metallic,—fit for loud laughter and piercing wail, and all that may lie between; speech and speculation free and plenteous ... very chaotic,—his way is thro' Chaos and the Bottomless and Pathless' (quoted Martin 1980; p. 242). The lines above from section XXXV of *In Memoriam* epitomize the Chaos, a chaos of language intrinsic to a chaos of meaning and identity. In this they summarize a dilemma that does not belong to Tennyson alone but to the whole tradition of Western metaphysics: 'If Death were seen / At first as Death, Love had not been, / Or been in narrowest working shut.' The spirituality of love and of the immortal soul are placed against the materiality of sex and of the death of the body. The central figure in this opposition is woman. As Simone de Beauvoir says, uncannily echoing Tennyson's words:

> [Woman] incarnates all moral values, from good to evil, and their opposites; she is the substance of action and whatever is an obstacle to it, she is man's grasp on the world and his frustration: as such she is the source and origin of all man's reflection on his existence and of whatever expression he is able to give to it; and yet she works to divert him from himself, *to make him sink down in silence and in death* [my italics] ... she is everlasting deception, the very deception of that existence which is never successfully attained nor fully reconciled with the totality of existents. (de Beauvoir 1987; p. 229)

There is a sense in which the dichotomy de Beauvoir describes is barely upheld in Tennyson. His anxious obsession with women and his increasing conviction of their polluted mortality become less and less able to support the notion of their immaterial potential. Perhaps the result of this is not merely misogyny but a threatened collapse of Western dualistic philosophy. If this collapse is an ontological dilemma the twentieth century is struggling to solve, it finds a prophetic articulation in the sexualized discourse of Tennyson's poetry.

Alphabetical List of References

Elizabeth Abel (ed.), 1982. *Writing and Sexual Difference* (Harvester: Brighton; University of Chicago Press: Chicago, 1980).

William Acton, 1968. *Prostitution [Considered in its Moral, Social and Sanitary Aspects, in London and Other Large Cities: with Proposals for the Mitigation and Prevention of its Attendant Evils,* 1857] ed. Peter Fryer (MacGibbon Kee: London).

W.H. Auden, 1946. *A Selection from Tennyson* (Phoenix House: London).

Nina Auerbach, 1982. *Woman and the Demon: The Life of a Victorian Myth* (Harvard University Press: Cambridge, Mass.).

Elizabeth Barrett, 1954. *Elizabeth Barrett to Miss Mitford*, ed. Betty Miller (John Murray: London).

Elizabeth Barrett Barrett, 1969. *The Letters of Robert Browning and Elizabeth Barrett Barrett 1845–1846*, 2 vols., ed. Elvan Kintner (Harvard University Press: Cambridge, Mass.).

Roland Barthes, 1979. *A Lover's Discourse: Fragments* (Jonathan Cape: London).

Simone de Beauvoir, 1987. *The Second Sex* [1949] (Penguin Books: Harmondsworth).

John Berger, 1972. *Ways of Seeing* (B.B.C. and Penguin Books: London and Harmondsworth).

Penny Boumelha, 1982. *Thomas Hardy and Women: Sexual Ideology and Narrative Form* (Harvester: Brighton; Barnes & Noble: NJ).

A.C. Bradley, 1902. *A Commentary on Tennyson's 'In Memoriam'* (Macmillan, New York).

Peter Brooks, 1987. 'The Idea of Psychoanalytic Literary Criticism', in *Discourse in Psychoanalysis and Literature*, ed. Shlomith Rimmon-Kenan (Methuen: London and New York).

Peter Coveney, 1967. *The Image of Childhood* (Penguin Books: Harmondsworth).

Carol Christ, 1977. 'Victorian Masculinity and the Angel in the House' in *A Widening Sphere*, ed. Martha Vicinus (Indiana University Press: Bloomington IN).

Terry Eagleton, 1978. 'Tennyson: Politics and Sexuality in *The Princess* and *In Memoriam*' in *1848: The Sociology of Literature*, ed. Francis Barker *et al.* (University of Essex, Colchester).

Sarah [Stickney] Ellis, 1839. *The Women of England, Their Social Duties, and Domestic Habits* (Fisher & Son: London).

Shoshana Felman (ed.), 1982. *Literature and Psychoanalysis. The Question of Reading: Otherwise* (John S Hopkins University Press: Baltimore and London).

Shulamith Firestone, 1972. *The Dialectic of Sex* (Granada: London).

Michel Foucault, 1984. *The History of Sexuality: Vol. I, an Introduction* (Penguin Books: Harmondsworth).

Sigmund Freud, 1959. 'Delusions and Dreams in Jensen's "Gradiva"' [1907] in *The Complete Psychological Works of Sigmund Freud*, vol. IX (The Hogarth Press: London).

Sigmund Freud, 1957. 'Mourning and Melancholia' [1915] in op. cit. vol. XIV.

Sigmund Freud, 1955a. 'The Uncanny' [1919] in op. cit. vol. XVII.

Sigmund Freud, 1955b. 'Beyond the Pleasure Principle' [1920] and 'Being in Love and Hypnosis' [1921] in op. cit. vol. XVIII.

Elliot L. Gilbert, 1983. 'The Female King: Tennyson's Arthurian Apocalypse', *PMLA*, 98.5, October 1983, pp. 863–78.

Sandra M. Gilbert and Susan Gubar, 1979. *The Madwoman in the Attic* (Yale University Press: New Haven and London).

Jennifer Gribble, 1983. *The Lady of Shalott in the Victorian Novel* (Macmillan: London).

Mary Jacobus, 1986. 'Is There a Woman in This Text?' in *Reading Woman* (Methuen and Columbia University Press: London and New York).

Myra Jehlen, 1982. 'Archimedes and the Paradox of Feminist Criticism' in *Feminist Theory: A Critique of Ideology*, ed. Nannerl O. Keohane, Michelle Z. Rosaldo and Barbara C. Gelpi (Harvester: Brighton).

W.S. Johnson, 1975. *Sex and Marriage in Victorian Poetry* (Cornell University Press: Ithaca).

Gerhard Joseph, 1969. *Tennysonian Love : The Strange Diagonal* (University of Minnesota Press: Minneapolis).

John D. Jump (ed.), 1967. *Tennyson: The Critical Heritage* (Routledge & Kegan Paul: London; Barnes & Noble: New York).

John Killham, 1958. *Tennyson and 'The Princess': Reflections of an Age* (The Athlone Press: London).

Melanie Klein, 1986. *The Selected Melanie Klein*, ed. Juliet Mitchell (Penguin Books: Harmondsworth).

Eve Kosofsky Sedgwick, 1985. *Between Men: English Literature and Male Homosocial Desire* (Columbia University Press: New York).

Julia Kristeva, 1980. *Desire in Language* (Basil Blackwell: Oxford).

Julia Kristeva, 1986. 'Freud and Love: Treatment and Its Discontents', Julia Kristeva, 1986. *The Kristeva Reader,* ed. Toril Moi (Basil Blackwell: Oxford).

Jacques Lacan, 1982. *Feminine Sexuality: Jacques Lacan and the École Freudienne,* ed. Juliet Mitchell and Jaqueline Rose (Macmillan: London).

Robert B. Martin, 1980. *Tennyson: the Unquiet Heart* (Faber and Oxford University Press: London and New York).

Eleanor Marx and Edward Aveling, 1886. 'The Woman Question', *Westminster Review,* 69 [January—April 1886, pp. 207–22].

John Stuart Mill, 1970. *The Subjection of Women* [1869] (with Mary Wollstonecraft's *A Vindication of the Rights of Women*) (Dent's Everyman's Library: London).

Kate Millett, 1972. *Sexual Politics* (Abacus: London).

Juliet Mitchell, 1984. *Women: The Longest Revolution* (Virago: London).

Ellen Moers, 1977. *Literary Women* (W.H. Allen: London).

T.H. Vail Motter, 1943. *The Writings of Arthur Henry Hallam, Now First Collected and Edited* (MLA: New York; Oxford University Press: Oxford).

Erich Neumann, 1972. *The Great Mother: An Analysis of the Archetype* [1963] (Princeton University Press: Princeton, NJ).

Keith Nield (ed.), 1973. *Prostitution in the Victorian Age: Debates on the Issue from Nineteenth Century Critical Journals* (Gregg: Farnborough).

Mario Praz, 1960. *The Romantic Agony* [1933] (Collins Fontana: London and Glasgow).

Ralph W. Rader, 1963. *Tennyson's 'Maud': The Biographical Genesis* (University of California Press: Berkeley and London).

Jane Rendall, 1985. *The Origins of Modern Feminism: Women in Britain, France and the United States, 1780—1860* (Macmillan: London).

Lillian S. Robinson, 1971. 'Dwelling in Decencies: Radical Criticism and the Feminist Perspective', *College English*, 32, May 1971, pp. 879–89.

Christopher Ricks, 1967. 'Tennyson's Methods of Composition', *Proceedings of the British Academy, 1966-7*, pp. 209–30 (London).

Christopher Ricks (ed.), 1969. *The Poems of Tennyson* (Longmans, Greene & Co: London and Harlow).

Christopher Ricks, 1972. *Tennyson* (Macmillan: New York).

Clyde de L. Ryals, 1967. *From the Great Deep: Essays on 'Idylls of the King'* (Ohio University Press: Athens, Ohio).

Susan Shatto (ed.), 1986. *Tennyson's 'Maud': A Definitive Edition* (The Athlone Press: London).

Hilary Simpson, 1982. *D.H. Lawrence and Feminism* (Croom Helm: Beckenham, Kent).

Alan Sinfield, 1986. *Alfred Tennyson* (Basil Blackwell: Oxford).

Lionel Stevenson, 1967. 'The "High-Born Maiden" Symbol in Tennyson' [1948] in *Critical Essays on the Poetry of Tennyson*, ed. John Killham (Routledge & Kegan Paul: London).

[Harriet Taylor], 1851. 'The Enfranchisement of Women', *Westminster Review*, 55, April—July 1851, pp. 289—311.

[Hallam Lord Tennyson], 1897. *Alfred, Lord Tennyson: A Memoir by His Son*, 2 vols. (Macmillan: London).

Peter Thorslev, 1965. 'Incest as Romantic Symbol', *Comparative Literature Studies*, 2, 1965, pp. 41–58.

Jeffrey Weeks, 1981. *Sex, Politics and Society: the Regulation of Sexuality since 1800* (Longmans: London).

Ann Wordsworth, 1981. 'An Art that will not Abandon the Self to Language: Bloom, Tennyson and the Blind World of the Wish', in *Untying the Text*, ed. Robert Young (Routledge & Kegan Paul: Boston, London and Henley-on-Thames).

Virginia Woolf, 1945. *A Room of One's Own* [1928] (Penguin Books: Harmondsworth).

Elizabeth Wright, 1984. *Psychoanalytic Criticism: Theory in Practice* (Methuen: London and New York).

G.M. Young, 1986. *Portrait of an Age: Victorian England* [1936] (Oxford University Press: Oxford).

Index